~~LESSONS OF DECAL~~

SOPHIE SEITA

Published 2023 by the87press
The 87 Press LTD
87 Stonecot Hill
Sutton
Surrey
SM3 9HJ
www.the87press.co.uk

Lessons of Decal © Sophie Seita 2023

ISBN: 978-1-7393939-0-8

Printed and bound by CPI Group (UK) Ltd, Croydon, CR0 4YY
Cover photograph: Sophie Seita and Simone Kearney, *Desire Lines*,
performance, Raven Row, 2019 (video still)
Design: Stanislava Stoilova [www.sdesign.graphics]

For Laura, for the decals of love that never lose their hold

Let it Percolate: A Manifesto for Reading

First presented at Brown University (*Translation Across Disciplines*, 28 February 2020) and Harvard University (*Contemporary Translation in Transition*, 6 March 2020), and subsequently published in *Bricks from the Kiln* 4 (https://www.b-f-t-k.info/).

Words can contextualise, embellish, explain. They can be raw, they can be tender, they can be violent. They can be matter of fact or they can translate matter into something else. Words force us to be nuanced.

'To translate is to surpass the source'—these are some words I put into the mouth of a character in *My Little Enlightenment Plays*, a performance project in which I rewrote, translated, responded to and, one could say, *corresponded with* some Enlightenment thinkers and writers.

(Isn't translation always the putting of words into someone's mouth, that someone sometimes being you?)

While translation trades in words, it also encompasses, for me, the moving of material from one place to another. Which is admittedly a broad delineation. But capaciousness can be a generosity. So. Translation might mean moving a language, an idea, an image, a material (like paper, fabric, or clay) to a known or unknown elsewhere, or it might mean transforming it into another form, genre, medium, or context.

This piece, which is a kind of delirious reading-in-progress, proposes a sprawling and lounging understanding of translation:

translation as an inventive, generative, and
   often collaborative practice;
translation as a movement *across*;
translation-as-writing-as-reading; and
translational reading as a pedagogical tool.

In other words, translation is in my 'feminist killjoy survival kit.'[1]
   'And so the three things I take to the Desert Island of

Obsessive Exercise are nuts for nourishment, hummus for humility, and dragon fruit for keeping the eyes alight amidst the non-variation and promise of paradise.'

—Which is another thing I put into a play. When I translate, I keep everything in play. Or at bay? Sound play, in turn, like any good tutor, imparts knowledge by osmosis.

Like a manifesto, I see translation as a deeply pedagogical form. Because it teaches you how to read.

So here's my manifesto for reading.

> Principle 1: No to verticality! Languages and art forms don't exist on a slope of significance.

> Principle 2: No to valorising originals. Which is an old hat in its critique but bears repeating. Yes to old hats.

> Principle 3: I will view translation as a process for transformation.

> Principle 4: I will remain open to my own translation.

> Principle 5: A translational pedagogy is a playful pedagogy.

> Principle 6: A playful pedagogy is unpredictable; I won't know where the ball will land or who, if anyone, will catch it.

> Principle 7: Scratch the house style.

These almost-wise and not-quite-adamant demands serve a

pragmatic truth. Which is provisional. And admits to not-knowing.

'[Not] knowing', as Jack Halberstam suggests in *The Queer Art of Failure*, 'may in fact offer more creative, more cooperative [and] surprising ways of being in the world'. Translation, like a manifesto, like pedagogy, flourishes with a delayed futurity. If this were a proper manifesto, or a classroom, I would invoke a 'we', a call for action.

What action is reading?

Taking a shower is an activity. Taking a bath professes not-doing. To write in the bath is to enter the jurisdiction of floating. Of idleness. Lisa Robertson's poetic she-dandy allows herself to pursue her thoughts languorously.[2] What knowledge does leisure afford?

When you work on a translation you do figure eights of reading. 'To rush it breathlessly through does very well for a beginning. But that is not the way to read finally.' Virginia Woolf is speaking about the need to re-read a novel here, but her comment also resonates with our critical desire to parse, to extract, to unearth, as a means to an end.

Is parsing always in cahoots with parsimony?

Avoid finality! Etc.

A non-extractive reading might be one that answers in *kind*: not by translation into a different discourse, but by using a creative circuitry of aesthetic kinship.

Writing-through-reading can mean taking it in, chewing it.

Letting it percolate.

I WANT A PEDAGOGY OF PERCOLATION!

In my teaching, I promote what I call 'translational reading', which tries to understand a text, a work, by doing something with it.

In my workshop 'Reading with Material', I usually give participants clay, string, paper, tape, differently textured fabrics, plastic bags, wire, old coat hangers, and whatever else I can find. I then invite them to encounter their chosen material, spend time with it, ask questions about its properties.

Touch is an invitation to explore and grasp and therefore to know and understand.

Here's Eve Sedgwick in her book *Touching Feeling*:

'To perceive texture is never only to ask or know What is it like? nor even just How does *it* impinge on *me*? Textural perception always explores two other questions as well: How did it get that way? and What could I do with it?'[3]

Sedgwick could be giving us a gloss for translation here. And also for epic theatre. Brecht wanted an engaged audience, inviting an interest in function and use. How could what we see on stage (which is a translation of one kind of reality) be different?

I want my students or workshop participants to play with the materials, to perform with them. Sedgwick again: 'to touch is always already to reach out, to fondle, to heft, to tap, or to enfold, and always also to understand other people or natural forces as having effectually done so before oneself, if only in the making of the textured object'.[4]

Impractically, that is unserviceably, this also leads me to ask, as Joyelle McSweeney asks: 'What regime does a work of art appeal to? Does the work of art appeal to a sensory, generic, or interpretive regime?'[5]

I take this question as a pedagogical and artistic principle. A principle for reading. Again, what would that mean *practically*? To practise is to repeat an exercise.

For McSweeney: 'Translation: the migrant of a very special nature. The filthiest medium alive.'

Laloo, the red wife, the hitchhiker, in Bhanu Kapil's *Incubation: A Space for Monsters*, is the migrant-as-monster: 'A monster is always itinerant'. If, as Kapil writes, 'Sex is always monstrous', her speaker spits out: 'I want to have sex with what I want to become'.

And, if becoming is always becoming-*with*, as Donna Haraway suggests, then we become monstrous in the act of translation.

The monstrous is a deviant form.

And if the monster is in some way de-formed, it draws attention to form as constitutive of its being. Etymologically, the monster *shows* and/or *warns*.[6]

Maybe the translation-as-monster expresses our fear of derivation.

An experimental translation, by contrast, derives a fair bit of pleasure from deviating from the norm. Irreverently non-literal, it only literalises its own demand for diversion.

It is demonstrative of a process of persistent re-reading. Which we could call a practice.

*

Jack Halberstam, in writing about disciplines, states that 'being taken seriously means missing out on the chance to be frivolous, promiscuous, irrelevant' (*The Queer Art of Failure*).

In critical writing we cite others to show our knowledge, our debts. To pay homage. To agree or disagree. To find lines of con- and divergence.

Translation is always a dialogue. So:

L: We illustrate, we dangle another voice off the end of our critical fishhook. Which might be a distraction. And an ethical conundrum.

S: What if the hook were not for catching fish but a cyborgian pirate prosthesis? The prosthesis is an extension of the body.

L: 'My body is an extension of my body' (Barbara Browning).

S: 'That's kind of like the dumb myth of freedom; go make our own laws and control our own ship.' (Kathy Acker)

L: Which is the utopian dream…

S: Do we dream of the ability to think endlessly, without ever reaching the point of exhaustion?

L: Exhaustion has its own internal rhythm. Anxiety is the carefully trodden path of my own pleasure.

S: Anxiety is a translational topos. That is: topology is the interrelationship and arrangement of constituent parts. The properties of an object that stay the same under the constant stretching, twisting, crumpling, and bending.

L: Is that what you mean by understanding a text by 'doing something with it'?

S: Force yourself to think onto the page or go off it. So you can be off. Be beside the point.

L: QUOTE 'Crusting, pushing, shifting, sliding through itself. Shearing away. [...] Something that huffs itself, form evaporating, changing, moulding' UNQUOTE (McSweeney)

S: If criticism is obsessed with quotation, a manifesto for reading ought to be a barrage. I don't want to bombard you.

L: Oh, please bombard me.

*

How do we hold another's idea? Dearly, surely, so we can turn words into lozenges in our mouth.

When my primary reader is YOU, my reading path leads to the you I address in private or the *you* I imagine in a sort of shadow-play public. Maybe reading is always the private dance of the author under the intimate gaze of the reader, or, as Rebecca Solnit writes in *The Faraway Nearby*: what is 'said to total strangers in the silence of writing ... is [then] recuperated and heard in the solitude of reading.'

*

No is the manifesto's supreme interjection. I accidentally typed *injection*.

Interjections convey a sentiment. Grammatically, an interjection is unrelated to any other part of the sentence.

(You see, this is still a sort of manifesto for reading by making my reading manifest.)

Anne Boyer reminds me—through reading—that 'The no of a poet is so often a yes in the carapace of no. The no of a poet is sometimes but rarely a no to a poem itself, but more usually a no to all dismal aggregations and landscapes outside of the poem.'

When we say 'no' where does the negation lead us? 'No to style', says Yvonne Rainer. A style of negation is also a style. Style comes from stylus which is a pen. Around 1700, choreography began to mean the act of notating a style of dance on paper. For me, a choreography of language is also about gesture and direction, about motion and emotion. About legible and illegible shapes. For example, I think about how Pina Bausch's dancers weave patterns into the leaves on the stage of her disturbing piece *Bluebeard*. Crunching. The women literally go up the wall. The dance makes visible a metaphor. A physical translation. So they hang, suspended, like crushed insects, dried on wallpaper.

Is this taking the movement metaphor too far? The transfer.

'No to moving or being moved.' (Rainer again)

Translation can be a 'no' to being physically re-moved from the borders of identity or nationality.

How many more metaphors for translation can we conjure up?

'Metaphors inflate at their own risk' (Iain Sinclair). I was told this. When I made a promise I didn't quite keep.

Ian Patterson asks us to 'think about what happens when I read a poem which is based in an act of translation which imagines text out of one existence and into another even as it writes. Not so much translating a poem as translating the reading performance of a poem into the world of another poem. The source text here is more than a source and less than a text, or maybe the other way round, more than a text and less than a source. Or maybe neither. [...] We might suppose that any act of reading a poem harms it: intentionally, or unintentionally, we wound, disfigure, or deface the poem as we read it because we hallucinate our sense of its sense. As Winnicott puts it in another context, "The fact is that an external object has no being for you or me except in so far as you or I hallucinate it, but being sane we take care not to hallucinate except where we know what to see."'

What would it mean to hallucinate the text, the other, ourselves?

To hallucinate is to go astray in thought.

Often when I teach, I do not know what will come out of my mouth.

Teaching is the translation of reading into a room. A thinking out loud into space, with a direct address. Into a temporary holding space for ideas. Both the avowed expert, the teacher, and the allegedly impressionable students perform that act of translation. We paraphrase a text, an artwork, into supposedly more palatable prose.

What makes a work, or language, palatable?

To call what I do translational is to take the word ending as a simile. When something is like translation it doesn't need to *be* it.

If no is the manifesto's pet word, then re- is translation's prefix par excellence.

Repeat. Return. Re-read. Re-write.

Re-, as Rita Felski and others have observed, captures a shift in our critical vocabulary that is less focused on the destructive or negating work of de- or un-. Re- can signal movement in time and space, amplification, iteration, and simultaneously memory *and* futurity.

In this realm of re-, translation-as-writing-as-reading is in a constant mirror stage of towardness and relationality.

This recognition can be joyous or judgemental.

*

Sometimes we feel overwhelmed by a task at hand. Sometimes breathing feels heavy. The limbs might go numb. Could the tingling hands be a symptom of the itch to produce, all energy rushing to the life-sustaining organs?

Are hands not life-sustaining?

What is the tingling effect of translational reading?

When something goes numb it is also hyper-sensitive.

Let's add a principle to this failing, flailing manifesto.

Principle 8: I am willing to care. And I am willing to show it.

---

[1] I'm borrowing the term 'feminist killjoy survival kit' from Sara Ahmed whose remarkable *Living a Feminist Life* (2017) has not only been an enabling influence on my book, but is also the first text I'd add to my survival reading list.

[2] Lisa Robertson, *Proverbs of a She-Dandy* (Vancouver: Morris and Helen Belkin Art Gallery, 2018).

[3] Eve Kosofsky Sedgwick, *Touching Feeling: Affect, Pedagogy, Performativity* (Duke University Press, 2003), p. 13.

[4] Sedgwick, p. 14.

[5] Joyelle McSweeney, *The Slavish Mould, the Filthiest Medium Alive: With Special Reference to Matthew Barney, Andy Warhol, and Divine* (Ugly Duckline Presse, 2012).

[6] The word 'monster' has two origin stories, according to which it's derived either from Latin *monere* (to warn) or related to *monstrare* (to point out, show).

Decals Of Love, Or, The One True Imposter
(A Lyric Lecture On/With Wendy Lotterman's Poems)

This piece was first given as a 9am lecture to undergraduate students at Cambridge in spring 2019, and then rewritten for *Manifold: Experimental Criticism*, issue 1 (2020/2021), edited by Emma Gomis and Jennifer Cookson. It was also presented as a live lecture at The Courtauld, at the invitation of Alice Butler, in May 2022, for '"What a Hazard a Letter Is": Correspondence in Feminist Art, Art Writing, and Art History'. Please note that all quotations from Wendy Lotterman's forthcoming collection *A Reaction to Someone Coming In* (Futurepoem, 2023) have been put in italics to mimic the experience of hearing the work performed live where a distinction between 'my' own analyses and reflections and Lotterman's poetic lines merged into one reading. In the live setting, all quoted lines by Lotterman were projected at the exact moment they appeared in my script. The poems referred to are draft versions of: 'Tie', 'Winter Noodles', 'Third Season', '≈ ≈ ≈', 'Equator', '≈ ≈', 'In the Flowers of Young Girls in Shadow', 'Intense Holiday', 'Powers of Ten', 'Sandals', 'Family Triage', 'Horses', and 'Lake Anza'.

Forms of Address

Dear Wendy,

I'm twirling like a leaf in the wind, feeling all the rich red and orange and burnt auburn; and even grey suddenly seems like an interesting colour. I'm soaking it all up.

Wish me luck that my emotional quandaries will somehow magically resolve themselves.

xxx

*

Love poem, a:

Definitions, just like descriptions, aim for greater and greater precision, encircling the object until it can be captured. They want clarity, a demarcation of outlines or limits. But in this desire for clarity, they invent roundabout ways of figuring out suitable forms of address.

In ON: *Contemporary Practice*, a print and digital magazine dedicated to discussions of 'one's contemporaries,' Thom Donovan and Michael Cross pitch their editorial model as 'motivated by desire, friendship, sociopolitical commitment, and discourse among one's communities and peers.' It's a motivation that leads me to a question about form: 'can we observe a present while it is still occurring; that is, before it has ossified into events consigned to a representative past?'[1] What form do we give this observational present?

I've written elsewhere about the 'movable contemporaneity' of provisional avant-garde communities.[2] Sometimes poems speak directly to a contemporary sensibility, aesthetic form, or content (like, the Internet), others rebel against such directness, transforming the frames that hold the poem along the way.

This lyric lecture deals with the indentations on the surface of our contemporary moment (my contemporary moment?) made by the poems of the American poet Wendy Lotterman. Always careful to follow the curves and contours, I will read Lotterman's work closely but also rovingly and lovingly. I love these poems. I am enamoured with them. This lecture is my attempt to make sense of my infatuation with Lotterman's words.

For a while now, some theorists have suggested that critique isn't the only form our writing about literary works could take. Critique as we have come to know it in close readings, for example, usually produces a response that follows the formula 'on the surface X looks like this, but really, if you lift the lid, tweak open the closet, the true meaning will be revealed' or it produces a slipshod cataloguing of formal features pointing everywhere and nowhere. At its best, however, close reading can be a *thinking-with*, an alongside, in delightful entanglement, thus staying true to the text's spirit, but also taking it as an occasion for going elsewhere.

Decoy1

Love poems in their simplest definition are poems inspired by—or in some obstinately stochastic way 'about'—love in all its multiple forms and addresses and conceptual caresses.

I put 'about' in quote marks because I am interested in prepositions, the work they can do. Love poems exist *around* or *near* a loved object; they're approximating it impatiently or perhaps somewhat hesitantly.

But love poems aren't just inspired by love, they can inspire love in return. I am going to be talking about both directions and relations here—their allure, their transactions.

Performatives, like 'I love you' are speech acts that often occur in transactional situations, easily tested by the addition of a 'hereby.' I hereby order you to do this. I hereby arrest you. I am arrested by these poems, which is a form of love. And love is a performance artist who can't get enough attention. Who demands a response. Like a decoy.

It is rather awkward to declare love and not receive a response. So Wendy Lotterman's poems have called out their love and I shall answer their calling. They weren't written for or about me, but I am, for the purposes of this lecture (and my life), claiming them for myself. And this is a key feature of the love poem, as much as for the love song.

We want to make it ours.

I will now copy for you one of Lotterman's poems in its entirety, a poem which I have made my own through reading.

I will then proceed to use her words to present my case, my
encomium, at Plato's notable banquet.

TIE

*The game cannot end in a tie, you say, as two
tears streak down each of your cheeks. A penalty
kicks out the window killing one of two twins,
leaving the other to receive her love in doubles.
What comes next. Freebasing hypertension and
soft pretzels as sudden death parts our hair in the
middle and we find this absolutely spectacular, the
way an answer comes forth from the woods. In
the video, we disappear back into the iridescent
leaflet of original suspense, reimbursing the worst
of what's kept to the breast. But sex is not a
mother unable to pick which kid she loves more.
One twin always dies since the game cannot end
in a tie. Two skies sitting in a tree, sequencing
love and contract. Two trees rejecting the room,
fucking beneath the sky. Skies indifferent to the
difference between one and two and two times
you tell me that one team has to win, halving
your cake as evidence of pleasure in domestic
measures and tan-lines scrawled across your
frosted hips, split in two even scenes of beauty
with bouncers announcing the border. The erotic
trespass expires by the time it's safe to cross. In
the yard, privates collide with wine and Scrabble
as I contemplate the single, silicone dome they
emptied on the belt at security. How to keep this
in perspective, myself, inadmissible to that love
or what happens on each side of the border. I
find it absolutely intolerable not to be in your*

bed, relaxing diaphragms and freebasing our
inseparable futures. I find it intolerable. Grieving
the national imperative to win, make rank, and
identify, or what TV calls victory and textbooks
call healthy development. But I would enter you
both until genealogy inverted if such love were an
appropriate taste. Sex and cat toys punctuate the
open-concept honesty of first nights at sea with the
fluency of decoys that don't get homesick. I got
lonely, cried in church, went to a concept hospital
for only hair and nails. Zionskirch[e] falls in and
out of relation, but only as long as you think it:
that this can and can't go on forever, that you do
and don't want this to go on forever, that you
are safe on planes, in the bathroom, imprisoned,
asleep, but that it is better to be outside, beyond
the idea of your secret interior. Banks break.
Wives break and begin again with a contract that
assimilates the doubt. The right reasons rain down
like documented angels with the safety of love
and statistically good looks. Your little rose wakes
up in Stella Luna's fleece with the epistemology
of horse girls gone wild. Her fruit-leather face,
their zero sibilance policy. The tribal-style corona
locks lips with the dream of a child who knows
what she wants before the dye sets. A freezed out
lucidity of basic instinct mixed with a minimum
of fear. The nightly tinnitus finds its way into
your life, into a locket between our breasts in
the bedroom where a shag-rug declares the space
between girlhood and universality. Nipples touch
the arch of your foot before your weight creates a
prepubescent girl. A key to that room is etched on
a single grain of rice that floats insensibly inside

a vile on your chest, bobbing with your body in
the water. There is a limited amount of faces that
you can remember, but the diaphragm still tries to
expand. Sudden death parts life in two scenes of
less an excess: why I love you specifically, and why
I can't cry for Argentina. I squeezed my thighs
tight so I wouldn't fall off. Like most protests, the
bruise will drain and then return to stasis. Feeling
redistributes on the left so that holidays on your
hip are spent without gifts. It isn't too late; you
are not behind because you choose what I chose
a long time ago and shame is not a baby in our
hand-me-down bassinet. Your dreams turn sweet
and then uncomfortably sour as sudden death
drafts two teams of unequal need. It's too soon to
give up. A golf-ball sized polyp moves into view
as I reason that it is too soon to give up. No to
this and all other metaphoric volumes arresting
the underdog's wire-coat momentum, like an
internalized doorstop lodged in the joint-birthday
of desire. Life is a bottom. Only I can take the
wind out of my sockets and trade gummies for
head in the underwater playroom. I find you there.
In a bulls-eye of kindness between fir trees and
mowed out rings of concentric tenderness. You
are soft and resonant. Your twin leaves the party
before you can do the same. Come out, bearing the
shape of the house that you came from. Arrive the
diner, rarified by light-years of desire. Metaphoric
volumes of moss will roll out, red hot along the
lava beside the road. There is a limited amount
of faces you can remember. There is a secret you
don't yet know how to confess. You close both
eyes, redistributing ghosts to the perimeter of your

sensory kingdom. Skies divide, the bed dissolves like dip 'n' dots. I find you there, in rings of concentric threat where the truth produced two wings of equal size. There is a limited amount of faces. I love you specifically. The game cannot end in a tie, but you are paralyzed by indivisible desire, and terrified by the loss of every side.[3]

Girls and Gemstones

A tie is a knot. Things get stuck.

Is post-shag-rug adulthood equivalent to the universal and the homogenous?

Love poems, which depend on the universal for their appeal to the reader, simultaneously depend on the specificity of the lover.

Wendy Lotterman's poems are not universal. The Universal kicks around as a ghost and causes a fuss—or is it the Specific? The specificity of 'you.' You as in you babe.

I love you specifically, but perhaps you are also a *lesser proxy* of my mother in this *replicable nursery*.

You sub in as an exit strategy. But people and situations aren't metaphors or instruments; they can be read both as symbolic and absolutely singular, which is the core of what constitutes an acute crisis in these poems. Full of ferocious frustration, something always remains unconsummated, unrealised.

The erotic trespass expires by the time it's safe to cross.

[W]here lanyard grants access to the gardens, is also where
*[p]ossibility lays flayed before our separate reservations as
range-of-motion invites the body to corroborate.*

And will it?

Passes expire. The lanyard might promise a garden of earthly
delights but it needs to be used at the right time, otherwise:
ingress deletes the actual arcade. Or, by entering you undo
the very idea of entrance, and thus *kill the mystery.* Maybe
you feel desire needs boundaries to flourish.

*There's a password for the party: it's the crevice where
histamine brings your body into knowledge.* If you let it.
The crevice is a hidden or unknown or unenterable space
that tickles or threatens you with an allergic reaction; an
automatic, impulsive response.

Desire can endure delay only so long. Eventually you need to
act: *you swear by the rate of exchange and the temperature of
two legs that must finally put the subject to bed.* The subject
matter or the lover? You can't decide so you return to the
obsessive Vitruvian escape room, hooked by mathematically
perfect proportions, idealised and therefore also *indecipherable.*

*I can't tell what the rivulets of impossibly soft access are
saying, but I get it.*

The speaker makes a decision and then questions it again,
sequencing love and contract (or con*tract*)—depending on
where we put the stress.

24

No, you cannot get back into the same bed you left. The real non-transferable ticket is you.

Lotterman's poems are full of dualisms. They describe the *binary siren of your nostrils*, or *two tears; two twins; receiv[ing] love in doubles; two trees; two skies indifferent to the difference between one and two.* The skies may be indifferent but the poem's speaker isn't. Nor am I. The addressed 'you' reminds us of the impossibility of evenness, that love will be divided, that you can't have your cake and eat it, too.

Barbara Browning, another connoisseur of sexy language, argues otherwise. Citing the cultural critic Lewis Hyde, she writes, 'In the world of gift ... you not only can have your cake and eat it too, you can't have your cake *unless* you eat it. [...] For Hyde, that's the link between the redistribution of wealth and eros. To him, and to me, the beauty of the gift is that, like sex, it confounds our sense of what it means to give pleasure and receive it. The more you give, the more you have.'[4]

In Lotterman's poem, the cake is halved.

Halving your cake as evidence of pleasure in domestic measures and tan-lines scrawled across your frosted hips, split in two even scenes of beauty with bouncers announcing the border.

For Lotterman, *feeling redistributes on the left so that holidays on your hip are spent without gifts.*

And:

You close both eyes, redistributing ghosts to the perimeter of your sensory kingdom.

Tan-lines also leave traces of liminality on the body, *announcing the border* that can or cannot be crossed. What pierces the back and forth between twos, between mirrors, is the *single, silicone dome.* The question is: *How to keep this in perspective*—where the deictic points to *myself,* the *erotic trespass,* or the remembered scene at the airport, and either I—or whatever *this is*—is *inadmissible to that love or what happens on each side of the border.* But it's also intolerable to be admitted, or not to admit to it, *the open-concept honesty of first nights,* or *first nights at sea,* which might make you sea-sick, or maybe they won't because you're fluent in the language of floating, of swimming along with *the fluency of decoys that don't get homesick.* A decoy is a duck at sea.

You better hold onto the railing.

I squeezed my thighs tight so I wouldn't fall off.

Holidays on hips are formally, acrobatically, effective in their strong declaration in the face of doubt or objection, but *[l]ike most protests, the bruise will drain and then return to stasis.*

The mind doth protest too much against the intensity of feeling. And isn't the hip holiday already a gift or does this nagging child also want memorabilia from a trip to the *beaches on Bergen?*

When *feeling redistributes on the left* it achieves greater social, but not emotional, equality.

In '≈ ≈', Lotterman writes: *most days I imagine myself wrapped around my mother's ankle, or one of several lesser proxies.*

Body parts and juices move from
hip
to lip
to camembert
from parts to
crushed particulars.

Lotterman's poems reinvent the blazon-like poetic cataloguing
that tradition has imprinted on us. Repeatedly, the lover is
inventoried, with ankles, thighs, chest:

the limit case is inevitably your belly-button.

In mathematics, the limit case surfaces when one or more
components of an object are at the maximum extent of their
possible variation. In the philosophy of science, it refers to
an earlier theory which becomes subsumed into a later, often
broader theory. It's a special case of the generic theory.

We usually read the specific for the generic. To justify it. Or we
posit the exception. I am not interested in drawing out the queer
bits of Lotterman's poems to suggest that we must always read a
writer through their marginalised identity. I want to talk about
these poems' queerness because it gives me joy, and because
my queer reading of these poems is conditioned by the queer
contexts in which I encountered them.

I felt and feel cushioned by Lotterman's words. How they
hold me, have held me.

Can you avoid psychoanalysing when you know the poet?

Once we enter the realm of professionalised education, we
are taught not to read for pleasure and rather to subsume

our pleasure into a sublimated critical distance, to historicise, to move away from straightforward value judgements. This becomes somewhat more complicated with contemporary work when we can actively shape not only the canon but also contemporary debates and feelings. What are we reading *for*? And what would it mean to read along *with* pleasure?

Lotterman's poems lend themselves to being read to a lover. As pleasurable prompts. For seduction. Which puts a different spin on the question of the avant-garde's often proclaimed desire for (or lack of) efficacy. Wendy's poems are very effective. Given that these poems are queer and they've been put to the test in explicitly queer situations I would say that they are therefore also socially effective, not just romantically.

Are we allowed to read and use our friends in this way? It's a form of homage—that would be the conventional and academic framework, but I am also making Lotterman's words mine by uttering them in a specific situation, which I would call a romantic situation. It's situational appropriation. It's the best kind of impersonation, via poetic language.[5]

Jonathan Flatley has claimed prurience as 'a critical mood', a form of recognition, of knowledge.[6] We could also say that queer prurience is delightfully non-productive or non-reproductive. Writing about Maggie Nelson's *Argonauts*, Flatley comments 'As a queer critical text, as a text about queer theory, the text is open to exciting its readers, it thinks its readers might want to be aroused in the midst of learning about queer theory, and that that arousal might itself be a point of queer theory, but, at some basic level it is also a way of caring about her readers by trying to help them shift their mood (in part by showing us how queer theory helped her to awaken in her own world a new mood, or mode of attunement, a new way of being-with). [...] Like Warhol, for Nelson this is a way of being – and helping us to be – "ablaze with our care."'

How do we write about fantasies in a poem? Is the critic supposed to translate and make something explicit? Do I list suggestive words—*fist, mucus, on all fours*?

After all, the belly and the belly-button often have directional force. They pull the speaker in all the *cardinal direction[s]*.

There's also a pull between mystery and revelation. Something unspeakable and something that cannot yet be named.

Now you kill the mystery between your belly and everything else.

But only so much. There's still an issue of legibility, of reading signs. Casting away doubt:

I can't tell what the rivulets of impossibly soft access are saying, but I get it.

There are ways of getting it that can't be articulated.

There is a secret you don't yet know how to confess.

'Without fantasy, there would be no love' (Lauren Berlant).[7]

≈ ≈ ≈

Love makes waves. A cliché is a cliché because it's so true it is embarrassing, excessive, inappropriate. Cliché is a term from printing: it's a plate with which to make copies; a decal.

'Most of us, given a choice between chaos and naming, between catastrophe and cliché, would choose naming. Most of us see this as a zero sum game—as if there were no third place to be: something without a name is commonly thought not to exist. And here is where we can discern the benevolence of translation' (Anne Carson).[8]

The double tilde in mathematics is the sign for almost-equivalence. A mark of suspension. An approximation.

Decoy 2

≈ ≈

Decals of love spit up the dial-tone like nylon prayer flags. You constitute at least one remaining stanza of attachment, putting the lyric on pause with the ethical bedrock of debt. It's nothing to be ashamed of. Her legs upset you, over and over again – a smooth olive tonic on the way to what you can't touch. I tried you back and got nothing but net-worth; your mattress filled with Camembert. I am perfectly turned on and shut down by the repulsive taste of cream. For instance: your thigh rips open the seminal juice box, splashing face-paint on the taboo of incest and sending my prize to the waiting room. Evening collects in the vending machines as the room somehow ricochets your mood. Hesitation escapes through a backdoor oasis in which nothing seems to matter as much as it does at home, or home seems to matter when you're gone. There is a line that can't be walked. From the streets to my desk, where I saved your iridescent headshots in a set. A menagerie of chopsticks tests the tenderness of stakes not drawn to scale. The miracle is mediocre and rare, specifically yours and everyone's. It's exactly what it looks like: most days I imagine myself wrapped around my mother's ankle, or one of several lesser proxies. Dreams down pay the balance of what can't be staged in life, where I imagine the force of synthesis to be stoppable by a single disposable contact lens, placed on the tip of a penis. Yours or mine. We keep switching places. How else to felonize the scoliosis of class, or have uncommon consequence in a zero-fault state? Very little happened in the time it took to pass from conditions of rain to snow. The sky opened up and watched us waste the day. A barely reflective stretch of cellophane takes your wavy portrait, but can't remember anything. It is exactly what it looks like. Our non-negotiables are fertilizer and an endlessly replicable nursery.

*

Sometimes we have to put the lyric on pause. You put romantic exclamation on pause because, perhaps, you're facing a dilemma, you're fighting over forbidden fruit or in this case: cream.

I gender the cream, the Camembert, the juice box.

I pretend to re-read my Freud, my Melanie Klein, my Jacques Lacan—what would they have to say to your fertiliser, your replicable nursery, this taboo of incest?

Finally, I love my therapist more than any other man; as soon as this is true, it no longer needs to be.

Transference is the redirection of feelings from childhood to a substitute, usually one's therapist in *stanzas of attachment*. Or it's the transfer of one love object to another. Perhaps, also, here, it's the surface transfer initiated by the decals of love, tattooed into habit, the movement from surface to depth that the poem so tenderly dramatises.

In your first draft of the poem, *fertilizer* was *tracing paper*, a material for replication. For tracing lines. For repetition. *Her legs upset you, over and over again.* I see the commentary on warped social stratification, *the scoliosis of class*, the *uncommon consequence in a zero-fault state*—which rightly argue that the same rules don't apply to everyone—but I zero in on what I can't touch, on her legs upsetting you.

Sometimes we have to put the lyric on pause. In order to read what's actually there.

And so I read this poem as if in *erotic lockstep* with your other recent poems. And then I learn that the poem isn't about *that* at all.

You ask if this throws things. I say no. This is perfect.

Having access to the poet's compositional motivations might throw a reader off. Or it might throw into relief the workings of a text in a new light. (In cliché printing there's a difference in level, which allows for the transfer).

This mis-reading either makes me a bad reader or a good friend. To encroach on the poem in this desirous way. Or maybe it makes me a good reader but a bad friend for not picking up on the biographical detail.

Do poems want to be fully understood?

I am not completely wrong; it just turns out that the love is of a different kind. A different register.

The poem's subtext is a sick parent. Suddenly I notice the mention of a *catheter*. The word *recover; the waiting room*; the question *why does it hurt you to move?*

You add more keys to the carabiner.

You see, this is also a lecture about the situatedness of reading. Would I have read this poem differently in the library rather than in bed and with company? The order of reading matters, too. Knowing that the poems 'Horses' and 'Sandals' are about a particular lover, I chased the love train of the other poems, too. I let myself be led in a particular direction, or rather: I leapt. Into that direction.

I.A. Richards chides me: 'And the feelings that rush out may take a course that is only partially directed by the poem.'[9]

We look for what we want to find.

Which is like love.

Maybe we want all poems to be love poems. Maybe we

want a poem to be the key to a new relationship or affair. Reading aloud or sending a poem as a gift is an incentive *for* love, the instigator *of* love.

I revisited these poems for this lecture and they hit me with all the force they did the first time I read them but now they're also couched in their specific romance, the specific inflection of their tangible impact on my life.

Enter Jonathan Flatley, reassuring the reader: 'it's entirely possible for a text to seem to "have" one mood, or "be about" one mood, and yet *produce* a mood in its readers that is distinct.'[10]

Enter Wendy: *No more clues.*

Enter Diana Hamilton, raising a toast:

> 'It's anti-intellectual to presume self-doubt means one hasn't thought hard enough;
>
> —everyone who's ever been smart at all—just like anyone who has ever really had faith, in God or in Love—is completely plagued by doubt.
>
> But still.
>
> I'm not sure the men watching know this,
> and I like to watch women
> be fucking masters of discourse.
>
> Unfortunately, or fortunately—I don't know how to say this part—I have to return to the part of that phrase that troubled you, if you read it carefully,

and has troubled me the most since I was a child, in love with women, in hate with myself:

I like to watch women.

Whether they're mastering their discourse or not, honestly.

But mastery isn't an escape from the question of sexiness; it pairs really well, in fact, with tousled hair.'[11]

Hamilton here gets at a conundrum of contemporary feminist and queer writing. There is both the desire to be accessible and boldly 'test the sponginess of explicitness' (to quote myself)[12] and foreground elements of identity and the body or, conversely, to embrace obscurity and abstraction, often associated with a male avant-garde tradition. This has been an ongoing debate for the feminist avant-garde since at least the 1980s.

Verity Spott illuminates both the pitfalls of binary thinking and of the desire to make one's identity legible in 'Against Trans* Manifestos': 'the observable is tenuous.'[13]

Description doesn't run along neat lines.

Caspar Heinemann agrees: 'Maybe sometimes all you can do is be the messy incoherent first draft you want to see in the universe.'[14]

As does Lotterman: *Now and then, portraits of young girls present two alternative futures in which I accept either the meltdown of mountaintop removal, or the secondary embellishments of Jello.*

Lotterman here references the American coming-of-age movie *Now and Then*. While one character binds her chest with tape, her friend stuffs her bra with pudding-filled balloons.

The choice is one between two poles: to exaggerate and emphasise, or to minimise and maintain. Both undo the artificial and natural divide.

Lotterman's poetry revels in such wobbliness.

The poem is also couched in the context of summer camp, which is referenced a few times throughout Lotterman's work, a spatially and temporarily contained microcosm for sexual development and where social pressures play themselves out.

For Sara Ahmed, '[b]odies become straight by tending toward straight objects, such that they acquire their 'direction[.]' [...] The 'nearness' of love objects is not casual: we do not just find objects there, like that. The very requirement that the child follow a parental line puts some objects and not others in reach.'[15]

Parental love is enormous and mistakenly cast as the foil to all future partners.

At first glance it seems like the more radical intervention in 'nature' is the mountain-top removal, but the Jello just hides its ethical (and oppressively gendered) footprint more sweetly and in an artificially coloured guise.

Ahmed again: 'Of course, when we inherit, we also inherit the proximity of certain objects, as that which is available to us, as given within the family home.'[16]

Objects and objectives. Materials and values.

Our non-negotiables are fertilizer and an endlessly replicable nursery.

The construction also appears in '≈ ≈ ≈': *Our non-negotiables are hardwood floors and strong family values.*

'We inherit ways of inhabiting and extending into space'[17]

—which shape what's present.

Calligrams of Absence

When Lotterman studied at Bard, she wrote a thesis titled 'Calligrams of Absence'. What she says about Mallarme could equally apply to her own work:

> 'The most honest testimony begins where it cannot be given. [...] The poet's failure to forge a link between language, the self, and the world results in work that bears witness to these ruptures. And yet, the confluence between the disruption of the poetic form and the poet's own adversity ultimately manages to create another link, as the poetry participates in the same conflicts experienced by the poet. The language points to what it cannot articulate by revealing the instances of its own failure.'[18]

Which we might call queer.

To substitute an absence.

'Sub' as verb and prefix appears frequently in Lotterman's poems.

Tagged by speed and free-play in this famously unbeatable level. We sub out.

Your knees sub in for the breeze.

Learning love on dummies with dad is the ruse of all workable substitutions.

But also: *In place of you, nothing.*

Substitution isn't so easy, after all. The lover is irreplaceable.

There is a stage at which the world empties out every proper noun and you, specifically you, sub-in as the tailored fulfillment of what life would like to bat next.

To sub is also to submit:

> *It's been so long since I had sex the way I wanted,*
> *except that yesterday I did, only after identifying*
> *the unquestionable ripple, and then submitting to the*
> *fortress of a fluke. I end with a Gettier, in which*
> *stimulation is an accident of my*
> *low threshold for pleasure.*

The Gettier problem tests our understanding of propositional knowledge. Justified beliefs based on sensory data might feel absolutely true, or are true by sheer luck, and thus trouble what we understand to constitute knowledge.

Somewhere in the middle of all of this there is a timeline of

fungible love in which I forgot to say that I couldn't come
home on half-days to find the light of two perverted suns
doing sex things on the bed since the golf-balls in my wallet
cannot feel or be felt.

Distractedly, I now think again of the 'ingress', and how the
sun makes an ingress into the cardinal signs at equinoxes
and solstices...

Life is a bottom, but sometimes we find *bottom[s] subtending*
tops, straight lines joined at a point, or a bract extending
under a flower to support and enfold it.

Perhaps I am also reading you for a theory of love.

I get on the couch with no intention to be legible.

The One True Imposter

We meet in a new scene of
reading where dawns of disco reflect the one true imposter

of equestrian sovereignty in the carotid body of water.
That gallop is you.

The lover is a contradiction in terms, *the one true imposter*,
but like the carotid arteries, the main vessel that supplies the
head with blood.

No Answer

Roland Barthes writes in *A Lover's Discourse*, in a chapter
on silence titled 'No Answer': 'The amorous subject suffers

anxiety because the loved object replies scantily or not at all,"
and then in parentheses:

> '(Like a bad concert hall, affective space contains
> dead spots where the sound fails to circulate. —The
> perfect interlocutor, the friend, is he not the one
> who constructs around you the greatest possible
> resonance? Cannot friendship be defined as a space
> with total sonority?)'[19]

We desire and give each other total sonority, tonal sorority.
We call each other honey to feel held. We affirm our desires
and encourage each other to pursue them. We comment on the
vertiginous vernality of the affair. Talk about metaphorical
proposals. Taking the tiniest of risks to test the waters.

Massaging balm into the desert's cracking theme, you get wet,
restless, head by the belly. In the dim-lit violet fish-shack, we
remain, for that moment, explicit.

And we refuse the accurate adjectives. Who cares what
restless could actually mean. The prettier words get at the
underside of things, a different form of truth. Or maybe their
surface sheen is just camouflage, which, when pierced, reveals
their utter correctness. Which you call overkill, I 'poetry.'

Does a love poem depend on the candid? Or on the candy?
Another decoy.

Our snack municipality is sweet and plainly impossible.

Perhaps our true task is to study *the supple science of a sweet*
indentured / future, where a gesture systematically melts you.

But extended explicitness is foreclosed because that would force a decision, an action:

True correlation becomes not really possible: bottom subtending tops, or the opposite, but not at once. Lips collapse into access without accent: siren of a superintended pleasure.

Pleasure *lives forever in that cognate promise.*

Let's try not to accelerate things. Decisions make you tired. But so does not-acting. Feelings take up mental space, an amorphous and non-coherent mesh; you can't articulate them.

I still see you, lounging on the floor at La MaMa Galleria, playing Karl-Marx-as-lapdog in my performance, my feminist utopia, asking me and the audience: 'what's up?' Sometimes we write lines already hearing, imagining, others saying them, thus writing an address without knowing it.

In an interview with Natalie Eilbert for the *Atlas Review*, you say:

> 'If I get any thrill from people reading me, it's probably secondary to an immediate blush. Or maybe it's thanks to it. As soon as I reveal something, there's an impulse to kick dirt back into the hole I just dug. But then there's also a competing excitement associated with the reveal, and even though I say 'competing' I think shame and thrill escalate together.'[20]

Which makes me think of projections and polarities and Philip Sidney who knew about both. His star-crossed lovers 'Astrophil and Stella' sigh:

from whose rules who do swerve,
Rebels to Nature, strive for their own smart.
It is most true, what we call Cupid's dart,
An image is, which for ourselves we carve.[21]

In other words, yes, our erotic worship is idolatry, a bit
fictitious, even selfish, who cares, it's pretty pleasurable!
'I think we all want others to usher us into the light, but I
kind of admire people who are like: fuck it, I'm not only
going to push the ouija piece (i.e. me), but allow others to
see me push it without shame.'[22]

Your love is also yours. You can own your desire. (But does
'own' imply ownership? And isn't that too simple, too much
like self-help?)

Indirectly and inadvertently Wendy's texts teach us, without
necessarily realising that proposition themselves, that there's
strength in expressing desire and asking for things.

And so in these poems, just as in real life, time passes.

*New guests confuse the tempo of the room. At this point
it's easier to just undress in the open-air jeep,
to reveal the dewy truth of music.*

I can't keep the rhythm, baby.

I can't make you representative, Wendy.

Of contemporary queer love poetry. Of the contemporary,
of queerness, of poetry, of love. And yet, I've chosen you,
you *specifically*, to be the paragon of our generation!

We still don't know exactly how the roads work, but it's okay.

Tetris

Reading Wendy's poetry is pure synecdochic pleasure.

Admonishing all lovers, Berlant writes: 'But we have already seen that your desire does not take you to its predestined object, the thing that will repair the trauma (of maternal separation, of sexual difference) that set you on your voyage in the first place. Desire is practical: it takes what it can get. Desire has bad eyesight, as it were: remember, that the object is not a thing, but a cluster of fantasmic investments in a scene that represents itself as offering some traction, not a solution to the irreparable contradictions of desire.'[23]

Or maybe: desire has great eyesight thanks to the proxy of the rosy tint, but has burnt its tongue from a scalding liquid, drunk too fast.

I still have a small but visible scar on my left hand from a tray of burnt nuts on that first night in Crown Heights with a rekindled romance of remainders that didn't add up. I don't need to analyse this. It's so overdetermined.

The bellies in the stadium collectively spell
what you already know: that our pre-symbolic crushing
is extinct, and is the only thing worth saving.

In the interview mentioned earlier, Lotterman continues:

>   [O]ne more thing, while we're on the lyric—
>   some of my favorite poets offer these sprawling,

panoramic views of cultural forces in intricate collision. Their poetry draws back to reveal the big picture of our time and place, like some fabulous, glitchy erector-set, too big to comprehend from within. I mostly don't do that. I go in. It's like that Eames movie "Powers of Ten", that zooms away from a couple lazing on a patch of grass in Chicago by powers of ten until our view is super-galactic, and then zooms back into the man until our view is sub-cellular. When you zoom into an individual—or, in the case of the lyric, the self—the subject *becomes* the panoramic, its own index of bigger forces, a complicated repository of an overdetermined "I" whose concerns are the sound of these forces clamoring. So I don't think expansive poems are disengaged with subjectivity, and I don't think lyrical poems are unexpansive.[24]

You go in.

In love you have to go in.

And then we realise that we have already said it all. In this or that poem. To this or that lover. It's a frustration we cannot get over.

My attempts to enter are redirected into
a growing portrait of increasing blurriness;
the roof of the building becomes
the Tetris of my wet desperation.
Privacy is a real thing, I guess,
too firm to be crushed by the waves of my soggy,
ambient love. I have already written this poem.

There are some poets who essentially write one long poem no matter what they write. In other words, they continue the thinking begun in one poem; they wrestle with one question; they write in one vein; it's one tonal constellation. I think Wendy Lotterman is one of these writers. Each poem is still distinct in that it broaches (on the surface) different topics or is shot into focus by an experience, but is ultimately an extended thinking into verse, spread out across her poems.

You say: 'I have trouble getting into short, punch-liney poems. [...] that sort of deadpan, monochromatic sincerity doesn't bowl me over. And of course I want to be.'[25]

What does it mean for a poem to bowl you over?

Work that creates 'that kind of fabulous combustion of thought that leaves me both winded and grateful.'[26]

In her feminist reading of Diotima's speech in Plato's *Symposium*, Luce Irigaray concludes her analysis like this:

> Neither the good nor the true nor justice nor the government of the city would occur without beauty. And its strongest ally is love. Love therefore deserves to be venerated. And Diotima asks that her words be considered as a celebration and praise of Love. [...] what she proposes to contemplate, beauty itself, is understood as that which confuses the opposition between immanence and transcendence. An always already sensible horizon at the depths of which everything would appear. But it would be necessary to go back over the whole speech again to discover it in its enchantment.[27]

*

Dear Wendy,

Yes to feelings as guests that one can properly address! It's
something you are very good at in your poetry—each poem
showcases its own 'victory of the particular'. I especially like
the new one you sent. I keep thinking about the choice you
set up between 'the meltdown of mountaintop removal, or
the secondary embellishments of Jello'. Both feel momentous
but also wobbly from tremoring (especially because of the l-
and m-sounds). I think there's something incredibly seductive
in your style—the suggestion of intimacy that is also partially
semantic, the revelation of some secret under various layers
of associative textual density or a kind of argumentative
logic that only really works in poems or in dreams. Your
poems often read themselves, psychoanalyse themselves, and
place symbolic footholds or hooks along the way, which
do not connect to a consistent metaphoric architecture and
that's nice. I love reading these poems as a way of thinking
through something—it's seriously good poetic thinking, i.e.
thinking that happens in poems because of their prosody,
their structure, their metaphoricity, and intensity. Your
poems are also instructive, but in an indirect way: neither
their instructions nor their poetic arguments are reducible to
one statement. They're also just fun. I will have to think on it
some more. I'd love to write about all this some time.

Love,

Sophie

[1] Michael Cross and Thom Donovan, 'About', *ON: Contemporary Practice*, [undated], <https://on-contemporarypractice.squarespace.com/about/>

[2] See Sophie Seita, *Provisional Avant-Gardes: Little Magazine Communities from Dada to Digital* (Stanford University Press, 2019).

[3] Wendy Lotterman, 'Tie,' *A Reaction to Someone Coming In* (manuscript, forthcoming with Futurepoem). 'Tie' previously appeared in *The Literateur* (2016). Other poems from this manuscript have also been published in various journals: 'Sandals' in *SAND: Berlin's English Literary Journal* (v. 18, 2019); 'Horses' in *Virgulentxs* (small-issue zine published by Lotta Thießen, Berlin 2018); 'Delete to Receive' in *Prelude* (v. 3, 2017); '≈', '≈ ≈' and '≈ ≈ ≈' published in *Poor Claudia* (2016); 'In the Flowers of Young Girls in Shadow' in *BOMB* (2017).

[4] Barbara Browning, *The Gift, or, Techniques of the Body* (Coffee House Press, 2017), pp. 6-7.

[5] To some extent we are always appropriating a poem when we read it out loud to a lover or friend or when we send it on a birthday card or read it at a funeral or a wedding or any other public or private occasion. This conundrum relates to my wider interest in repurposing as an aesthetic and what it means creatively and ethically to 'make something mine'. What changes when you play with or absorb or recontextualise the words of someone you know, someone you're close to? At the same time, I also want to tug at the cliché of the lyric poem—that this 'I' or 'you' is a shifter and can be occupied by anyone. Not everyone occupies this I / you equally, because the poem is of course also couched in other discourses and structures of power. I'm always curious when a work contains very specific references that resemble an artist's life and yet are also fictional and must be read beyond biography. Then again, I'm here playfully suggesting that as a friend you might be forgiven for reading a poem autobiographically—against your academic training or your better judgement.

[6] Jonathan Flatley, 'Prurience', Critical Moods Panel, MLA Annual Convention, January 2017, <https://supervalentthought.com/mla-17-643-moods-of-criticism-theatrical-humorless-prurient-susceptible-alacritous/>

[7] Lauren Berlant, *Desire/Love* (Punctum Books, 2012), p. 69.

[8] Anne Carson, 'Variations on the Right to Remain Silent', *Nay Rather* (Paris: Center for Writers & Translators, American U of Paris, 2013). Also available online here: <http://artandcrap.com/ensayos/anne-carson-variations-on-the-right-to-remain-silent/>

[9] I.A. Richards, *Practical Criticism: A Study of Literary Judgement* (Harcourt, Brace, 1929), p. 61

[10] Flatley, 'Prurience'.

[11] Diana Hamilton, 'Essay on Bad Writing', in *God Was Right* (Brooklyn: Ugly Duckling Presse, 2018).

[12] Sophie Seita, *Emilia Galotti's Colouring Book of Feelings*, in *My Little Enlightenment Plays* (Pamenar Press, 2020).

[13] Verity Spott, 'Against Trans* Manifestos', *Datableed*, 3 (2016), <https://www.datableedzine.com/verity-spott-against-trans-manifestos>

[14] Caspar Heinemann, 'NOTHING ELSE BUT: Some Fragments Written with the Intention of Becoming Something More Coherent at a Later Date Despite Experience Exposing This as Unlikely', *Interjection Calendar*, 004.08 (Montez Press, 2018), [p. 10].

[15] Sara Ahmed, *Queer Phenomenology* (Duke University Press, 2006), pp. 86-87.

[16] Ahmed, p. 86.

[17] Ahmed, p. 86.

[18] Lotterman, 'Calligrams of Absence' (2012), *Senior Projects Spring 2012*. 11.<https://digitalcommons.bard.edu/senproj_s2012/11>

[19] Roland Barthes, 'No Answer', in *A Lover's Discourse*, trans. Richard Howard (Hill and Wang, 1979), p. 167.

[20] Wendy Lotterman, 'A Conversation with Wendy Lotterman', interview by Natalie Eilbert, *The Atlas Review*, 31 March 2014, <https://theatlasreview.wordpress.com/2014/03/31/a-conversation-with-wendy-lotterman/>

[21] Philip Sidney, *Astrophil and Stella* (1554–1586).

[22] Lotterman, 'A Conversation with Wendy Lotterman'.

[23] Berlant, p. 76.

[24] Lotterman, 'A Conversation with Wendy Lotterman'.

[25] Lotterman, 'A Conversation with Wendy Lotterman'.

[26] Lotterman, 'A Conversation with Wendy Lotterman'.

[27] Luce Irigaray, 'Sorcerer Love: A Reading of Plato's Symposium, Diotima's Speech' / 'L'amour Sorcier: Lecture de Platon, Le Banquet, Discours de Diotime', *Hypatia*, 3.3, French Feminist Philosophy (Winter, 1989), pp. 32-44 (p. 44).

Vulva's School: A F*cking Didactic Take on Experimental Feminist Performance Art, or, How to Read

for E. W. W.

This piece is adapted from a 50-minute-long lecture performance of the same title, first presented at the University of Cambridge in November 2018, and then re-staged at the independent art space Florens Cargo in Darmstadt, Germany, in August 2019, and at Jawaharlal Nehru University (JNU), New Delhi, in January 2020. In all three iterations, the performance was accompanied by a slide show of images and videos. The second and third performance further added costume, choreographed movement, voice recordings, and several props (a skip rope, a red suitcase, a red wig, school props like a slate, a ruler, and some chalk, and one 'my little pony' figurine). In 2020, I was commissioned to turn the lecture performance into a video piece for the online exhibition #*WIP: Work in Progress/ Working Process* (October 15, 2020–January 15, 2021) curated by Tuna Erdem and Seda Ergul (Queer Art Projects), together with guest curator Sarah Hayden. Four video stills from the piece are included in this chapter. An extract of my text was published in *Humanities Provocateur: Towards a Contemporary Political Aesthetics*, ed. by Brinda Bose (Bloomsbury, 2021). Slide show images have here occasionally been replaced with a description in italics.

An artist in a black kimono, her arms lifted and angled to frame her head, index and middle finger pressed together in a salute of scare quotes. Between them a line of text, luring us to 'Pretend you are not there.'[1]

I'm on my way back from a movement class, mulling over the ideas that came to me as I was twisting and bending my body, looking at the other participants in the room, mostly actual dancers, also bent backwards or upside down. And so united in our joint upside-down-ness we were perhaps the right way up. Perhaps, I thought to myself, this is an homage to Madeline Gins and Arakawa's vision for a Reversible Destiny, the art-architecture-poetry-imagination project which proposed that changes in bodily perception would lead to a change in consciousness. I type these notes frantically on my phone on my walk back to Anna's apartment, so as not to forget the lines I've been saying as a little tune in my head, but also because my fingers are frozen since New York has gone from 16 degrees one day to -3 on another, and I'm half-kicking myself for not obeying my New Year's Resolution to not text while walking.[2]

OK. So here we are. I started this piece, this public demonstration of a private investigation, with a little autobiographical preface, a curtain-lifting ice-breaker which is always a good way to create intimacy with an audience, isn't it. Of course, this narrative anecdote could have been entirely made up. In this case, its purpose is simply to give the *impression*, we could say an *illustration*, of the personal. And it's reasonably believable—I could be this character—I used to live in New York, I visit regularly, I love exercise. But:

'the formation of a hypothesis is senseless
conveys the banality with a touch of mystery and excitement.'[3]

As a matter of fact, I detest simple autobiography, but I have a soft spot for self-reflexivity, thanks to my long-term heroines Kathy Acker and Christine Brooke-Rose. They obsessively commented on their own act of writing, like so: 'This writing is all just fake (copied from other writing) so you should go away and not read any of it.'[4]

Copy that.

The overt presence of the performer in writing is thematically apropos. Because today I will not just talk *about* feminist performance art but will occasionally perform for you the bridge between art and scholarship. Over the last few years, I have become increasingly interested in merging creative and critical discourses, an experiment that finds a good home in the format of the lecture performance. I consider the lecture performance a live essay but not necessarily in the form of an essay. This fascination emerges from a longstanding interest in appropriating and translating various—often historical—source materials in my performances. To create a multi-vocality. To make language material. To be choreographed by language.

Describing one of Ellie Ga's lecture performances, Emmy Catedral suggests that '[h]er hands over the projector lens become the key performers.'[5] More broadly, I would say: the projector is the lecture performance's easel. Layering and associational logic are its procedures. So, lean back. Let the language wash over you. Let me lecture you. Which, going back to the Latin roots of the word, simply means: let me read to you. Feminism is, after all, a fairy tale. Or rather: the tooth fairy may in the end be a feminist conceptual artist, gathering your teeth for her army of biting.[6] We could say this is the feminist genius: giving a gift, a coin, a smile in exchange for a weapon. As Sara Ahmed says in *Living a Feminist Life*: we all need a feminist killjoy survival kit.

In what was perhaps the first ever feminist lecture performance, Virginia Woolf told the students at Girton and Newnham in Cambridge that we think through our mothers when we are women. Today, we would qualify that we may have 'many-gendered mothers' (as Maggie Nelson notes—via Dana Ward) or feminist, queer, trans, and non-binary artists *as* mothers or *instead of mothers*. To counter the 'procession of educated men', we need other lineages, other pedagogical strategies.[7] We have never had a Vulva's School—where 'vulva' is anything but essentialist and rather a metaphor for a possible anti-patriarchal gender-abolitionist counter-institution.

Vulva's School is the title of a lecture performance by the American feminist artist Carolee Schneemann, whose work centred on the body for the almost 60 years of her career. In *Vulva's School* (first performed in Vancouver, 1995), Schneemann stands behind a lectern, wearing two gloves, one is a dog, the other a cat, with which she mimes a conversation, while reading a 45-page essay about semiotics, Marxism, and religion, which, she posits, has been rejected by various journals. The gist is: 'Vulva goes to school and discovers she doesn't exist…'[8]

*

A gaping mouth…
A fossilised idea…
A decorative motif…

*

Similarly, in her artist book *Vulva's Morphia* published the same year and going over similar territory (1995), we follow a character called Vulva, who learns quickly that she is not part of the curriculum: 'Vulva deciphers Lacan and Baudrillard and discovers she is only a sign, a signification of the void, of absence, of what is not male…'[9] Vulva's educational journey is complemented by images of female genitalia, sometimes photographic, sometimes symbolic.

There's something dated and second-wavy about all these vulvic symbols, of course; but there's also something energising about Schneemann continuing her practice and her emphasis on 'vulvic space' as an alternative knowledge space until her death in March 2019. Perhaps what's energising is simply her shameless *persistence*. And sometimes the past exerts power over us precisely because it's anachronistic, outmoded—in the guise of what Elizabeth Freeman calls 'temporal drag', 'with all the associations that the word drag has with retrogression, delay, and the pull of the past upon the present.'[10] Or maybe because Schneemann reminds us that we can use the body against the imposed limits on 'the body'. Eileen Myles recently wrote in 'The Cunt Speaks' for Schneemann's Barbican exhibition catalogue (2022): 'That act, to unravel the scroll from inside to *unroll my cunt*, that's what she's doing, making the inside out, kind of a trans act if you think of it, turning a cunt into a dick and, one more step, destroying art.'

In another performative lecture—*Mysteries of the Pussies* (1998)—Schneemann writhes on the floor on a podium at the Porin Taidemuseo in Pori, Finland, sometimes draped over the curator who awkwardly responds to images of Schneemann tongue kissing her cat *as well as* trying to stay on top of Schneemann's simultaneous live lecture on historical obscenities. In this as in other pieces, Schneemann's feasting on excess, on the indecent, on the monstrous, the messy, the dirty, the embarrassing and on the ageing female body is radical. Pleasure becomes a technique.

As Lisa Robertson puts it in *Proverbs for a She-Dandy*: 'menopause turns females into dandies. Some of our organs become purely self-referential. They have no further potential for family or spectacle or state: they're outside every economy. So now their meaning is confected in relation to convivial and autonomous pleasure only.'[11]

In what is perhaps Schneemann's most well-known lecture performance, *Interior Scroll*, she reads from a scroll she pulls from her vagina. She reads to us. She lectures us. In the script, Schneemann describes how she once met a 'structuralist filmmaker' who instructed her that her films were full of 'PERSONAL CLUTTER | THE PERSISTENCE OF FEELINGS', 'DIARISTIC INDULGENCE', and 'PAINTERLY MESS.'[12] So she took the knife aimed at her back and made it into an aesthetic. Indeed, Schneemann often blended the diaristic mess with a critical discourse that was folded into the poetic material itself—humorously, knowingly, dexterously. In the lecture performance *Americana I Ching Apple Pie*, performed at the Kitchen in New York in 2007, Schneemann prepares an apple pie in front of the audience, while also framing her action as a work of performance art. She opens by saying 'we have to think of the apple pie in terms of its art historical components. [...] the technique I'm going to show you is going to keep you so close to your art process.' She continues, while sloppily cutting up apples, chucking a bag full of flour into a big bowl, making a real mess: 'while I'm doing this, I should revisit the Marxist aspect, the labour involved.' She announces that she would like to have her own TV show, which would have to be called: 'deconstruction for the postmodern artist trapped at a dinner party.'

During that same New York trip mentioned earlier, I finally saw Judy *Chicago's Dinner Party* at the Brooklyn Museum— an epic feminist installation piece that sets the triangular table for 39 mythical and historical female figures at a ceremonial banquet to celebrate their contributions to history. *Dinner Party* exemplifies an effort in 1970s feminist art to share ideas and skills as part of anti-patriarchal pedagogy. Chicago and Miriam Schapiro also set up what we could call an offshoot of Vulva's School in 1971: the radical and short-lived Feminist Art Program at CalArts. I'm interested in these alternative forms of education that might 'teach us to transgress' as bell hooks puts it. And where does that interest lead me?

I'm thinking specifically about what bell hooks says about the merging of theory and practice and the need for a passionate pedagogy: 'What forms of passion might make us whole? To what passions may we surrender with the assurance that we will expand rather than diminish the promise of our lives? The quest for knowledge that enables us to unite theory and practice is one such passion. To the extent that professors bring this passion, which has to be fundamentally rooted in a love for ideas we are able to inspire, the classroom becomes a dynamic place where transformations in social relations are concretely actualized and the false dichotomy between the world outside and the inside world of the academy disappears.'[13]

*

A dinner party in the author's garden, with a plate laid out for the special feline guest, gazing into the distance. 'The Cat is My Medium.' The Auteur Behind the Scene in the Garden Academy.

*

In her 2013 video essay, *How Not to Be Seen: A Fucking Didactic Educational .MOV File*, critic and filmmaker Hito Steyerl offers a satirical take on the instructional film genre.[14] Steyerl's video is a sort of copy or creative re-imagining of the Monty Python sketch 'How Not to Be Seen', which pretends to be a government video about how to make yourself invisible in a landscape.

What's so fucking didactic about Steyerl's piece? Well, couched in the language of didacticism, the video is structured around five lessons for disappearing. It instructs you in the art of making yourself invisible. Who wouldn't want that?! For Steyerl, to become invisible in today's media landscape means to dodge the cameras and the video thus comedically intersperses green screens and airfield resolution targets. A computerised voice-over chimes disinterestedly other suggestions for 'how not to be seen', namely: to camouflage yourself, to become smaller than a pixel, to live in a gated community, to become a superhero, or to be a woman over 50. Another is simply to walk off screen. This reminds me of the ultimate act of performance art by the American conceptual artist Lee Lozano, who made a piece that exists only as a title and a commitment. In *Dropout Piece*, the artist removed herself from the art world and thus moved herself into obscurity. Like the unruly school dropout who no longer wants to play along.

*

The artist-as-teacher demonstrates 'camouflage' didactically by smearing computer-animated green cream on her cheeks, like a beauty mask, like war paint, for the resolution target.

*

There is, of course, something neurotic about this focus on visibility. The theorist Sianne Ngai has even called paranoia a specifically feminist affect of our times.[15] Steyerl's video satirically reveals that paranoia but never teeters on the edge of neurosis itself. 80s synthesisers lend a retro vibe. We end on a neat dance routine by the pixels. And Steyerl disappears.

The feminist and queer artist is usually already invisible. Or, as Eve Sedgwick notes, much violence is hyper-visible and ubiquitous—it needs no laborious detection—so what does exposure or paranoid reading add to that recognition?[16] And to be invisible as a female, queer, trans, migrant, disabled person, and person of colour, can often guarantee safety.[17]

Lately, I've been thinking a lot about teaching, about reading, how to put into words for myself and for others what a work does, and especially what feminist and queer work does. How to make sense of texts and performances, without sense-making being another manipulative imposition on me, the text, my readers, or my students, but where sense radiates from a spectrum like distributed particles of light, colour, or sound.

And of course, the truth is, I still often don't know how to read.

What I learnt from Steyerl through humour (sometimes the best kind of teacher) is that perhaps the format itself can be didactic. Like the MOV file. Can the form of this lecture performance be instructive, too? I wrote to someone recently that I rarely make mistakes. It wasn't exactly a lie—it was partly aspirational, partly a playful provocation. As in, bring it on.[18] Perhaps this 'bring it on' is a feminist gesture.

> *the loop of that which was just described or named is*
> *endless perhaps a square is there a square that is not*
> *dull what would it take to make it like it was a knife*[19]

Can you sing

To copy and remake, to re-read, is a signature feminist practice; but the signature requires repeating in order to be recognisable as such; and given that feminism has centuries of materials to catch up on, that scribal scratching into the groove of an alternative history might take some more time.

Don't despair, my friend tells me in a dream, repetition is a juicy democracy.

Sometimes we repeat things because we want to make them ours. Sometimes because we hope that by repeating we make them different. Repetition can give presence.

The supposed familiarity of the feminist gesture is sometimes pointed out to chide the feminist performer. Perhaps she's called Vulva or maybe she's called A One-Trick-Pony, which is her glittery code name. She is told that sexiness on stage combined with difficult language is 'expected'. She is told that to wear lipstick and heels during a performance is a concession to the patriarchy. She is told 'you don't need that', meaning: the feminist or queer label, or: the constant critique.

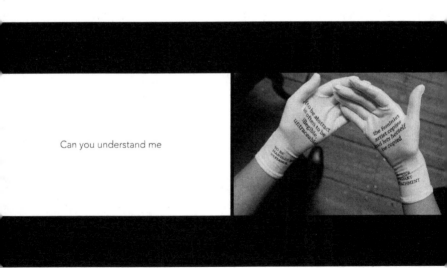

Can you understand me

\<dialogue\>

i: hello.
Pony: hello.

i: let's do that again.
Pony: ok.

i: hello.
Pony: hello.

Pony: different?
i: maybe.

i: i've forgotten the instructions.
Pony: that's sad.
i: it's not real.
Pony: ah.

*

it's an easy gesture, i use it often and expertly
i have no such options with the pony

*

we could call this pony's table talk
we all know that animals perform heroic deeds
and ponies are divinatory, they warn of danger[20]

*

Can you not vary it

What makes something a feminist or queer performance? Is it when someone who identifies as feminist or queer makes work, or if they depict feminist or queer subjects and cultural references? Gordon Hall calls this 'the glitter problem. Or the leather problem, [...] [or the] 1970s-crafts [...], bodies and body-parts, blood-and-bodily fluids problem.'[21] Instead, Hall proposes something like 'queer abstraction'. I like the sound of that.

To be abstract is often to be illegible. And to be illegible is often to be invisible. The invisible artist may 'flutter around the canon' but as such is, like a mosquito, a disturbance to the equilibrium, establishing the sting as her oeuvre.[22]

In queer time, Jack Halberstam argues, 'repetition is privileged over sequence.'[23] *The Queer Art of Failure* proposes a 'low theory' as a 'mode of transmission that revels in the detours, twists, and turns through knowing and confusion and that seeks not to explain but to involve' and that considers 'getting lost over finding our way'.[24] I'm deeply attracted to this lure of getting lost and also deeply scared of it. Theoretically, this is all very well, but practically it sounds a bit like the self-help book a well-meaning friend gave me for my birthday. What's more, how would we teach the detour?

Maybe this brings us back to form.

Maybe I'm reading too much into this.

Maybe this is just about throwing in a little bit of that good-old modernist fragmentation.

Can you understand me

What is the role of autobiography in teaching? This is a lecture after all! I have been influenced by the pedagogy of hospitality offered by feminist magazines like *HOW(ever)*, *HOW2*, and *Chain*, all of which featured experimental formats like the forum, or unusual introductions to works, as ways of figuring out how to do feminist theory in practice. Their pedagogy was one of active listening. These magazines set up a provisional school for writers and artists in their pages.

What does it take to found a school? A school of fish is a critical mass. A school of fish may seem choreographed but is not. A school of fish is a school of queer learning. In the Disney film *Finding Nemo*, Halberstam argues, 'Dory [as a queer subject] forgets family and tradition and lineage and biological relation and lives to create relationality anew in each moment and for each context and without a teleology and on behalf of the chaotic potentiality of the random action'.[25] A forgetful character like Dory disregards oedipal and heteronormative patterns and in a radical gesture of

65

self-re-creation also changes their own identity. Active forgetting, for Halberstam, has the potential to unfix fixed histories of oppression. Forgetting is a queer tactic. It's a way to turn away from expected lines.

*

A line shimmies 'just keep queering' as we swim into the lossless format. Half static, half moving, a gif animates ideas, flushes them out, and they slide in imitation, with ease.

*

What are our materials for learning? What do we hold onto? What do we cross out?

Classrooms often present learning like a detective drama. There's a riddle, a mystery, a puzzle to be solved, with the teacher or professor as hero(ine), and the students as side-kicks.

Vulva's School, by contrast, follows what Raul Ruiz says about his experimental film *The Hypothesis of the Stolen Painting*:

'As a rule, in a detective film, as in any gothic system—like Marxism or psychoanalysis—at any rate, in a system where there is a façade and inside a riddle, you enjoy finding the explanation. In a more baroque system, as in the system of Hypothesis, you don't enjoy finding the enigma. But rather go from one level of interpretation to another. It's like the horizon: once you reach the horizon, there's still [another] horizon.'[26]

Up until recently, every talk I would give, every performance, would be meticulously planned. I would know exactly what

I was doing and where I was going. I was over-prepared. But lately, I've started to explore the resourcefulness, even the lucidity, when I have not yet worked it all out, when I am not in top form (I've had a pinched nerve in my neck for three weeks now. How would we read *that*? Maybe queer performance is a form of shouldering. ALWAYS KEEP YOUR SHOULDER TO THE WHEEL.)

A provisional feminist pedagogy does not promote intellectual laziness or dilettantism, far from it. It's a serious attempt to experiment with forms of writing, making, and relating that allow us to think differently. It means setting up situations and phenomenological conditions that then determine newly what we can think, make, or say.

This may entail a certain vulnerability.

Who does and who does care

A how-to manual for Vulva's School:

If they say we write in milk, let them have our toxins.[27] Tipp-ex is our new fountain pen. The pupils at Vulva's School will wield it.

The labour of blanking out what was written before is not new, but Vulva's pupils do not need to be new. The gesture of re-, of re-writing, re-doing, re-making, is a crucial feminist tool. But after graduating from Vulva's School, even the prefix re- will be an archaeological relic. Always having had the patriarchal bone to pick, Vulva's pupils will have other, less unrelenting nourishments to chew on.

Vulva may be the headmistress, but there shall be no rulers,

*only triangle rulers. No straight lines. To think in the manner
of Vulva's School is to think in tangents, curves, slopes, and
angles.*

Drenched in correction fluid.

Tipp-ex to erase the 'tippen', the typing.

*But in English 'to tip' is to topple, to tip the scales, to throw
off the balance.*

Or:
It's tipping it down
Or:
I'm standing on my tippy toes
Or:
It's on the tip of my tongue
Or:
It's the tip of the iceberg

*And the tip is where we take the patriarchal, racist,
transphobic rubbish.*

*

In some ways, I have now arrived at a proto-type for Vulva's
School. A proto-type is all about experiment. It's about trial
and error, the renewed, the modified. It's about a model. It's
about the provisional. And it's about making and unmaking
types. It's also about the physical and material contact of
subjects and objects. What kind of knowledge we want to
impart. As artists, as writers, as teachers. And if we can
ultimately separate our identities so very neatly.

This could be a resolution.

Steyerl's AI instructor advises: 'resolution determines visibility. Whatever is not captured by resolution is invisible.'

> *the loop of that which was just described or named is endless perhaps a square is there a square that is not dull what would it take to make it like it was a knife*[28]

*

> *Another artist is seen holding a knife.*[29] *Her eyes are bulging silver balls or maybe orbs. Shimmering with the threat of patriarchal triumph.*[30]

*

Feminist and queer performance art is often angry, dissident, or emerges from dissatisfaction while its form may be utterly joyful, even exultant. The feminist killjoy is 'willing to cause unhappiness' and refuses to make happiness her cause, as Sara Ahmed gleefully suggests. She is recalcitrant.

Which is fucking didactic. A didactic take is a handling technique. Grab it.

I gestured towards this anger by using the expletive in my title, but by citing Steyerl it's already copied and transformed. And, of course, the expletive is also simply an intensifier. It adds affective force.

As Holly Melgard reasons in her performative text 'Holly Melgard Reads Holly Melgard': 'I make poems as readings—not poems to be read. Why wait to be asked before speaking? […] Why wait for an established person to solicit, welcome, and/or legitimate this work prior to permitting it to occupy public space-time?'[31]

A task I like to set my students is to write a short creative piece about a favourite artist or writer who influenced them, in a form that copies their style, as an homage that thinks through their work. Seduced by the exercise, I wrote in my notebook:

My Maya Deren is the Maya Deren of Meshes of the Afternoon. My Maya Deren is grainy videos on Ubuweb. My Maya Deren is a half-read chapter in JD Rhoades's book on Deren. What does it mean to write about an artist I don't really know; to claim her as mine? As an undergraduate I briefly kept a 'free writing' diary, following the advice of a tutor. In it, I would often write down my dreams. And then I stopped keeping the diary and I stopped remembering my dreams. Last night I dreamt I survived a plane crash. This now has a time stamp. My best friend Ayla and I were on our way to New York. There was so much space and air. Interestingly, my dreaming self did not experience any physical sensation of descent, of impending death, no pulling in the stomach. The descent was slow. There were big windows. We landed in water. We both said Oh shit. There was no impact. It was like 'the idea of a crash'. It was very conceptual. Even in the dream I liked that about it. I recognised the aesthetic gesture. I remember sighing Oh we're back. I regretted the wasted time more than anything. We left the plane. There was no drama. As I said, it was like a conceptual artwork. The dreaming dictionary says surviving a plane crash means that great things are on the horizon. Phew.

Is this a tangent? Or is this my Maya Deren?

There's always a gap between experiencing the vivacity of a dream and the prosaic narrative when you relay it afterwards.

A dream is also a bridge.

My body sprouts mushrooms, yellow red orange maybe mauve (?) (I like that word), surreptitiously sandy petals. They grow from my hips, my lower belly, slowly covering my entire body. I turn my wrist and moss traces my veins, bursting green lines, like hair to be pulled, or a tape strip to establish boundaries. Moss is for mothers.

My Maya Deren is also my translation of Uljana Wolf's 'Messages from a Beehive', which begins each paragraph and almost every sentence with 'My relationship with Belarusian is this' or 'My relationship with Belarusian is that'.

My Maya Deren is also repetition.
My Maya Deren is Anne Teresa de Keersmaeker's Fase.
My Maya Deren is also My Duchamp.
Or rather: My Duchamp became My Maya Deren.
My Maya Deren became my Theresa Hak Kyung Cha.
My Maya Deren has inadvertently become a list poem.
Anaphorically incantatory.
My Maya Deren shan't be edited (a lie).

My personal pronoun is an 'intellectual' investigation...To leave out pronouns would either be called the work's radical undoing of gender or the very absence of pronouns would be seen as a failure to be visible.

At a symposium in Santiago de Chile in January 2019, the poet and scholar Andrea Brady told the audience that as a young writer she used to leave out her subjectivity in poems, and that she did so with force and repetition; it was 'tyrannical'. I wrote that down afterwards. 'Tyrannical'. And added 'self-editing'.

At a Q&A after a lecture performance at the Royal Drawing School, I am asked who my influences are. I say something like the above but not in these words.

My Maya Deren is now also a chronicle of my reading and teaching.

*

So this lecture performance is then a series of propositions; maybe lessons, with the lesson yet undetermined. So you learn the steps.

*

Two women spin, fast, in sync, and then they're out of it, ever so tauntingly close. Four movements to find their shadowy other. Come Out. *Figures repeat. Accelerate, decelerate. Minimal shifts bring boundless variations, relations. Of what is turned and returned. Embodied abstraction and refined complexity.* To Show Them.[32]

*

Who makes who makes it do

Brent Hayes Edwards argues that 'there is something like a queer practice of the archive' that celebrates the 'elusive' and 'what can't quite be explained or filed away according

72

to the usual categories.'[33]

Is the elusive necessarily queer? Is queerness elusive? And do I want that? Except abstractly, except formally, but not in my body?

Recently, I've been trying to figure out how to 'have' feelings in writing. How can the ornamental, the voluptuous, go deeper than the sonority of the aphoristic, and how can abstraction be other than the cooler underside of the lush particular?[34]

We, as readers, as writers, have of course imbibed that form and content are inextricably linked, various 'extensions' (Creeley/Olson) or 'revelations' (Levertov) of one another. And yet, most talks and essays hop happily from a to b to c, with maybe some u-turns for kicks but even those are folded into a nice little argumentative trajectory. This is where the lecture performance enters stage left, flamboyantly donning a ruff or jabot, probably no tie.

*

Sophie Seita reads Sophie Seita[35]

action choices:

avoid the truth
avoid delicate matters
avoid being tracked down

instead chew up and spit it out
then carry out an important mission

a pony is queen of delicate matters
and says, i shall not cut through the fog love the world
be suitable

and the pony leaves to examine its folly, to excite someone,
to go where no man has gone before,

it induces, it listens, it rattles up some shit,
can't have it both ways,

> Pony, liberating the oppressed, jumps at chances,
> picks out the jewels in its crown, for it wears a
> crown, having killed the queen and stolen her
> ornaments. jewels in hands, or rather hooves,
> the pony leaps, and disperses the riches, puts the
> world in order, sings charitable progress, this is no
> exaggeration.

Pony is victorious. the pony has no record of losing.[36]

I'm citing myself again. Some would say, I'm running out of
ideas. I call it recycling. Or being in analysis. So language
can become modular. A form of transference. Which is all
about knowledge.

ACT III: I mean what I say.[37]

I want to move back in time briefly, to the progenitor
of literary and page-based performance: Gertrude Stein.
Another one of my teachers of reading.

In 'An Exercise in Analysis' (1917), the character called
'Part XXVIII' asks, but without a question mark: 'Can you

understand me.'[38] To which Act II replies 'I can understand you very well' which in turn is picked up by Act III merely rhymingly spinning the language in a new direction 'Do you agree with Miss Crutwell.' Whoever Miss Crutwell is, she is not in the play.

Humour undercuts any attempt at psychologising even the most abstract of characters.

    Act II
It was a copy.

    Act III
It was a copy.

    Act IV
It was a copy.[39]

One could snicker at this and say, well, is this repetition warranted, what's all this sing-song, but when the three copies are followed by Part XXXVII's admonition: 'Do not make a mistake', I am somewhat appeased. I remind myself that it is an '*Exercise* in Analysis' after all. And all exercise requires repetition.

*

The performers-as-pixels pirouette, cheerily chorusing 'When Will I See You Again.'

I mean what I say

---

[1] Hito Steyerl, *How Not to Be Seen: A Fucking Didactic Educational .MOV File* (2013).

[2] Perhaps an alternative tune can be found in Lisa Robertson's description of the menopausal flaneur: 'As she drifts, she hums a little tune. What is that tune.' Lisa Robertson, *Proverbs of a She-Dandy* (Vancouver: Morris and Helen Belkin Art Gallery, 2018), p. 25.

[3] Sophie Seita, 'Pony: Five Tableaux', *The White Review*, vol. 16 (2016), p. 16.

[4] Kathy Acker, 'Translations of the Diaries of Laure the Schoolgirl', in *Hannibal Lecter, My Father*, ed. by Sylvère Lotringer (New York: Semiotext(e), 1991), pp. 104-113 (p. 104).

[5] Emmy Catedral, 'Ellie Ga's Square Octagon Circle', *Bomb*, 143 (4 April 2018), <https://bombmagazine.org/articles/ellie-gas-square-octagon-circle/>

[6] I here wish to acknowledge that I have been inspired by my former student Desmond Huthwaite who wrote an essay for my class titled 'How to Bite: Experimental Women Writers and their Teeth'; a how-to guide to a new feminist aesthetic: an aesthetic of bite.

[7] Virginia Woolf, *Three Guineas* (Harcourt, 1938), p. 62.

[8] Carolee Schneemann, *Vulva's Morphia* (New York: Granary Books, 1997), unpaginated. *Vulva's Morphia* began as an installation of 36 images with text, <http://www.caroleeschneemann.com/vulvasmorphia. html> The text also appeared in *Sulfur*, 42 (Spring 1998), 14-21; and in *Women & Performance: A Journal of Feminist Theory*, 14.2 (2005), 51-53. A video of her performance is available though Electronic Arts Intermix.

[9] Schneemann, *Vulva's Morphia*.

[10] Elizabeth Freeman, *Time Binds: Queer Temporalities, Queer Histories* (Durham: Duke University Press, 2010), pp. 62-64, 70.

[11] Lisa Robertson, *Proverbs of a She-Dandy*, p. 2.

[12] Carolee Schneemann, 'Interior Scroll', in *Carolee Schneemann: More than Meat Joy*, ed. by Bruce McPherson, pp. 234-39 (p. 238).

[13] Bell hooks, *Teaching to Transgress: Education as the Practice of Freedom* (Routledge, 1994), p. 195.

[14] Steyerl, *How Not to Be Seen*.

[15] Sianne Ngai has suggested that 'confrontation with complicity becomes the specific form "paranoia" takes in women's writing'. See 'Bad Timing (A Sequel): Paranoia, Feminism, and Poetry', *differences*, 12.2 (Summer 2001), 1-46 (pp. 7-8).

[16] See Eve Sedgwick's chapter 'Paranoid Reading and Reparative Reading, or, You're So Paranoid, You Probably Think This Essay Is About You', in *Touching Feeling: Affect, Pedagogy, Performativity* (Durham and London: Duke University Press, 2003).

[17] See also: Verity Spott, 'Against Trans* Manifestos', *Datableed*, 3 (2016).

[18] Sara Ahmed, *Living a Feminist Life* (Durham and London: Duke University Press, 2017), p. 267. I also want to thank Raphael Lyne for telling me about the film *Bring it On* (2000), dir. Peyton Reed, written by Jessica Bendinger, which subsequently made it into this lecture performance.

[19] Sophie Seita, *Objects I Cannot Touch*, video (2014).

[20] Originally published in: Sophie Seita, 'Pony: Five Tableaux', *The White Review*, vol. 16 (2016).

[21] Gordon Hall, 'Object Lessons: Thinking Gender Variance through Minimalist Sculpture', *Art Journal*, 72 (2013), 46-57 (p. 47).

[22] Christine Brooke-Rose, 'Illiterations', in *Breaking the Sequence: Women's Experimental Fiction*, ed. by Ellen G. Friedman and Miriam Fuchs (Princeton: Princeton University Press, 1989), pp. 55-71 (p. 65).

[23] Jack Halberstam, *The Queer Art of Failure* (Durham and London: Duke University Press, 2011), p. 119.

[24] Halberstam, *The Queer Art of Failure*, p. 15.

[25] Halberstam, *The Queer Art of Failure*, p. 80.

[26] Raúl Ruiz, 'Two Comments on Hypothesis of the Stolen Painting', *Raúl Ruiz Dossier* (Sydney: AFTRS, 1992), p. 2. [Translation from 'Camera Je', May, 1979]. Quoted in Michael Goddard, *The Cinema of Raúl Ruiz: Impossible Cartographies* (London: Wallflower Press, 2013), p. 46.

[27] See: Denise Riley, 'Milk Ink', in *Selected Poems* (Reality Street, 2000), p. 104; and Lisa Robertson, 'Toxins', in *3 Summers* (Toronto: Coach House Books, 2016), pp. 19-30.

[28] Sophie Seita, *Objects I Cannot Touch*, video work (2014).

[29] It's perhaps not surprising to find so many knives in feminist art; most notably in Martha Rosler's *Semiotics of the Kitchen* (1975), but also twenty years later in Patty Chang's *Melons* (1998).

[30] I'm thinking of a scene in Maya Deren's *Meshes of the Afternoon* (1943), in which Deren faces her sleeping double, and just as she is about to murder this domestic version of herself, the woman wakes up, the perspective shifts, and we see her husband towering over her. The film ends with the husband returning home, finding the suburban housewife having slit her throat.

[31] Holly Melgard, *Essays for a Canceled Anthology* (Troll Thread, 2017), p. 9.

[32] See Anne Teresa De Keersmaeker, *Fase, Four Movements to the Music of Steve Reich* (1982).

[33] Brent Hayes Edwards, 'The Taste of the Archive', *Callaloo*, 35.4 (Fall 2012), 944–72 (p. 970).

[34] Sophie Seita 'My Little Enlightenment: The Plays and Textual Performances of Sophie Seita, interviewed by David Spittle', *3:AM Magazine*, 29 May 2017 <http://www.3ammagazine.com/3am/little-enlightenment-plays-textual-performances-sophie-seita/>

[35] This is an adaptation of Holly Melgard's brilliant title 'Holly Melgard Reads Holly Melgard' which I take as a model for thinking about self-reading.

[36] Originally published in: Sophie Seita, 'Pony: Five Tableaux', *The White Review*, vol. 16 (2016).

[37] This and the previous sub-headings ('Can you sing', 'Who does and who does care', 'Can you understand me', 'Can you not vary it', 'Who makes who makes it do') are from Gertrude Stein, 'An Exercise in Analysis', in *Last Operas and Plays*, edited by Carl Van Vechten (Baltimore: Johns Hopkins University Press, 1977) pp. 119-138; and from 'Four Saints in Three Acts' (1927), in *Last Operas and Plays*, pp. 440-80.

[38] Stein, 'An Exercise', p. 129.

[39] Stein, 'An Exercise', p. 131.

[Reading-in-Progress]

This addendum was included alongside Vulva's School as part of the exhibition #WIP: Work in Progress/Working Process, October 15, 2020–January 15, 2021, curated by Queer Art Projects (Tuna Erdem and Seda Ergul), and guest curator Sarah Hayden.

Vulva's School: A F*cking Didactic Take on Experimental Feminist Performance Art, or, How to Read is both the work and preparation for (the) work.

Here's Roland Barthes (translated by Kate Briggs) in *The Preparation of the Novel (*a pedagogical experiment in the form of several lectures about the plans for his unwritten novel):

'There is an age at which we teach what we know. Then comes another age at which we teach what we do not know; this is called research.'

We could also call this a way of reading.

My *Vulva's School* is a somewhat similar pedagogical experiment. It is based on a lecture performance first presented at Cambridge, where it emerged from a graduate seminar I taught on 'Experimental Writing by Women', in which I very much wanted to figure out how to teach what I did not yet know or what I knew but wanted to teach differently or unknowingly; to welcome vulnerability, uncertainty, and forms of thinking for which you cannot quite be prepared. *Vulva's School* is therefore dedicated to the students of that course.[1]

I then performed the piece in a slightly different version at the independent project space Florens Cargo in Darmstadt, Germany, as part of a city-wide arts festival, and again at Jawaharlal Nehru University in Delhi, just days after violent attacks on students and faculty following their peaceful protests against a fee hike of 150% imposed by the university administration.

Every context and occasion inflected and will continue to inflect the piece and will leave a mark on my own interpretation of it.

This is how I have announced the performance previously: 'Thinking about (and through) Carolee Schneemann, Hito Steyerl, Judy Chicago, Jack Halberstam, Gordon Hall, Lisa Robertson, Gertrude Stein, Maya Deren, Sianne Ngai, and Eve Sedgwick, but also about pedagogy, about my own teachers of reading, about abstraction and autobiography, about alternative forms of learning and relating, about pinched nerves, about visibility, about vulnerability in an institution, about detours, getting lost, but also being addicted to slickness, and as always (always) about serious copying and necessary (even inexorable) repetition.'

As a piece *about* process (of learning, of reading, of making), it also formally reveals its own process of being made. It wears its intellectual and creative debts on its sleeve. It reads itself. I read myself. I wanted the video, and the split screen in particular, to capture this multi-directionality and to represent my episodic, associative thinking.

One of the characters in *Vulva's School*, my alter ego, Pony, was originally conceived as a video in response to Raul Ruiz's *The Hypothesis of the Stolen Painting*, a sort of art-historical who-dunnit, an experimental film that sits between scholarship and speculative fiction, in which an art collector and his invisible interviewer try to find the link between a series of paintings and the sacrifices of a cult. To prove their hypothesis, they stage a number of *tableaux vivants*. There's a riddle at the heart of Ruiz's film. In that sense, it's related to teaching and scholarship. The scholar or student as detective. The text or artwork as mystery that can either be deciphered or proliferated. After watching the film in 2015, I expressed a wish to make a new video in which there would be no visual tableaux but in which they'd be merely described. I was and continue to be committed to the specific forms of thinking that are possible through poetic description. How a poetic text can make an argument, indirectly, provisionally, by encoding itself. I am fascinated by oblique angles. A descriptive language that is precise yet evasive. I never made the video. 'Pony: Five Tableaux' exists as an abstract feminist Sisyphus-myth published as poetry. So in *Vulva's School*, I return to this vision from several years ago, but incompletely, and in a new guise.

That maybe already gets at the heart of my mode of working. I rework a lot. So that, as I say in the video, 'language can become modular'. Why should we not return to the same language, hold it to the light, view it sideways, upside down, squintingly or extremely closely. For Etel Adnan, for Cezanne, and for numerous others, a mountain can become the same reference point over and over again.

I just remembered that there's a quote in there from yet another earlier piece of mine: 'The loop of that which was just described or named is endless perhaps a square is there a square that is not dull what would it take to make it like it was a knife', a text for which I *did* make a video, *Objects I Cannot Touch*. The loop of it made it into this piece, too.

In short: I'm thinking about the ongoingness of language. Its recyclability. A way of keeping something active, rather than 'done'. It's an obsessive return to materials previously used. To rehearse. In another text, I say 'I am so unrehearsed'. Which is anxiety speaking. You practise for perfection. I'm usually over-prepared. When I first wrote this lecture performance, I felt radically under-prepared. In the Q&A after the first iteration, a friend teasingly called me out on my polished performance of the *idea* of unpolishedness. And they asked me, What would the unpolished Sophie actually look like? Touché.

The thing is once you go down the road to slickness, the horizon gets pushed further away each time.

Slickness and messiness—the dual push and pull between my perfectionism and my desire to be surprised, to be led by uncertainty, messiness, vulnerability.

I am an obsessive editor; I go through numerous drafts. I think through writing. I also 'basically think through other people's language' as a character in another of my performances says. I think on and with the page.

I've come to realise that my readings and re-readings are often multiply mediated. How, for example, I have read one author through the eyes of another, or one artist or theorist through the lens of a teacher, a friend, a student. If there's one thing I wish for this piece, as perhaps for all my work, it is to give a semblance of the process of reading, with all its distracted *and* focused, specific *and* speculative powers. Probably everything I've done in the last four years can be boiled down to this promise: how a performance or installation can be a form of reading. How can I make an audience feel as if they were reading even though they're not? Does that make sense? I keep trying to articulate it to myself. I might need several attempts.

So how do you show process? If I were to give a representative image of this particular work in progress it would have to include all my readings, my re-readings, my mis-readings, my missed readings, all my multiple drafts. But even the technically in-process work would suggest a teleology towards the finished work or would certainly be read as a 'salient' example.

In every performance, every reading, a piece evolves. Each is part of the non-linear development of the story of my reading. My thinking about these issues hasn't ended. Just as I returned to Pony and keep returning to the same literary and theoretical texts, I will probably return to this lecture performance. The video is a snapshot of where I'm at right now. I might be tired of it one day, but I'll probably continue to grapple with its provocations, its ongoing temptations.

I will cite myself again and rewrite myself into and out of this reading.

---

[1] Having been taught an almost exclusively cis white male canon (with the occasional and exceptional 'woman writer' thrown in), I designed the course 'Experimental Writing by Women' because it was the kind of course I desperately craved as a student at Cambridge myself. Taking inspiration from Sara Ahmed's citational practice in *Living a Feminist Life*, the syllabus did not contain any work by straight white cis men. At the same time, I wanted to question and expand the very term 'woman' (against patriarchal belittling, and importantly, against TERFs claiming ownership over the category). As a class, we wanted to problematise the labelling of, say, 'women writers' or 'queer artists' in order to take them seriously as artists and thinkers beyond their identity category; at other times, an explicit exploration and interrogation of feminist and queer politics, aesthetics, and sociality helped us understand how a particular artwork or artist worked. We treated identity categories, like the concept of 'woman', as a 'real abstraction' (as Maggie Nelson calls it) which remains 'expansive and alive', 'in flux', and yet is 'not without real referents or pragmatic power'. We also read Andrea Long Chu's 'On Liking Women (The Society for Cutting Up Men is a rather fabulous name for a transsexual book club)' for the first session, which set the tone for our enquiries.

My Lazy Laboratory

This piece was commissioned by Yates Norton and published in the first issue of *The Rupert Journal* in January 2021, available here: <https://journal. rupert.lt/>

glide

I want a lazy laboratory. I want an abstract space and concrete place for experiment without yet knowing where I'll end up. In many ways that's the very definition of experiment, from the Latin *experior*, 'to attempt' but also 'to experience'. An experiment can in itself be an experience, rather than just a conduit for it.

But in writing, in art, in relationships, even Experiment is her own little bureaucrat. And for someone living in fear of its actualisation, laziness has the appeal of diving with sharks. You can be enamoured with the idea of languor but not with its practice. Say, you're on holiday somewhere sunny and humid and when you ask the owner of your little guest house what there is to do apart from going to the beach, he says: not much; just relax; feel the heat. You might reasonably or not so reasonably panic.

So sometimes you just land somewhere. You find yourself in a place that falls *into* place. Falling into place is an action that requires acceptance. A downward gesture, a drop into cushions, a sound of soft suction, like drawing an imaginary line down your windpipe; or the pleasure when things fit, when the deck of cards glides into its case or a sliding drawer clicks shut.

laziness in a new key

A couple of years ago, I began to fantasise about an alternative school in the form of a lazy laboratory, a languorous salon, in which 'menopausal she-dandies' (Lisa Robertson) and 'feminist killjoys' (Sara Ahmed) could 'teach [us] to transgress' (bell hooks). What would we transgress?—our imbibed desire for order, clear directions, strong work ethic, rigour, and individual genius. Instead, we'd celebrate collaboration, listening, care, and play—of variable rhythms, meandering directions, loops, and returns.

Let me present to you my pitch, my melodic invitation to tune in.

In the laboratory, we would practise a kind of doing that is about responsiveness and openness, about tuning in as a state of being attentive. We would query our impatience and welcome sleepiness, not to discredit the fiery rush of restlessness or the kick of precision but to expand our emotional palette, our vocal range, for thinking and making. As creative practitioners, we often have to justify what we do, be legible, find labels for our practice. In a cultural moment in which we're under the regime of excessive celebration of self-image, of daily documentation, of either stark or faux-nonchalant professionalism, we might want to get stuck a little, be a little confused, even delirious, like when we're sick. Give our eyes some soft focus. In a languorous state, we take pleasure in dreaming, inactivity; we let things happen, which is necessary for collaboration and experimentation. Laziness and languor etymologically signal exhaustion, weakness, faintness. So a lazy eye, a sluggish movement, might offer a different organising principle for the body. Sometimes your body doesn't work the way it's supposed to and sometimes you actively resist what it means for something to 'work'. For that not-working to work we need others in the room. We sometimes wouldn't know what to do, what to say, but we would be reassured by the poet Nisha Ramayya's invitation to 'not know together'. We would drum along to Raphael Sbrzesny's teaching style in the form of a 'polyphonic studio', a term he borrows from German theatre scholars David Roesner und Clemens Risi for non-hierarchical co-creation. Polyphony recognises difference. It's several voices coming together, harmonically interdependent.

I have experimented with some of the above ideas in a number of practice-based workshops, sometimes under the rubric of 'Reading with Material'. These workshops were driven by a recent inspiration (Pauline Oliveros) and a long-term inspiration (the singing method I learnt at the Lichtenberger® Institute of Applied Physiology of the Voice in Germany), and were focused on movement, writing, and some simple voice work.

Here are some of my questions and prompts:

> Voice exercise 1: Imagine your tongue is a dolphin. Your nervous system will know what to do with that image. It will translate it. Now speak or sing or hum with that image in mind.

> Voice exercise 2: Remapping organs. Walk around the room and imagine your feet have ears. The larynx and the ears are twins; both vibrate at high frequencies. Can you imagine your larynx with ears? Do the ears have a larynx? Can your ears give up a habit?

> 'The ear is a faithful collector of all sounds that can be gathered within its limits of frequency and amplitude. Sounds beyond the limits of the ear may be gathered by other sensory systems of the body' (Pauline Oliveros).[1]

> Movement or voice prompt 3: The tongue, the tips of our fingertips, and the soles of our feet have a

tendency to become soft. All sensory organs want to experience softness. There are floral principles in the receptors of our fingertips. Now allow these receptors to be oriented towards resonance, towards vibration. The vocal chords have a similar sensitivity to our fingertips. Can they have an encounter that resembles the receptivity of our sensory organs, a sort of self-touch? Our habits and our drive towards discipline and achievement limit our sensory awareness, bodily experiences and expressions of ease. Instead, let's ask ourselves: What happens when nothing happens?

pliable

In each of these exercises, I asked myself and the participants to observe the experiment with curiosity, free from judgement.

I also invited participants to bring a material and to explore that material's characteristics, its textures, what response it asks of us.

Here's Anni Albers in *On Weaving*:

'Concrete substances and also colors per se, words, tones, volume, space, motion — these constitute raw material; and here we still have to add that to which our sense of touch responds—the surface quality of matter and its consistency and structure. The very fact that terms for these tactile experiences are missing is significant.'[2]

What adjectives would we use for our material? Is it chewy, bendable, pliable, or wiry, or perhaps brittle, or permeable;

is the surface burnished or grainy or dull? Suddenly we're in the realm of poetry. What kind of knowledge can this encounter, this touch produce?

In *Touching Feeling*, Eve Sedgwick suggests:

'To perceive texture is never only to ask or know What is it like? nor even just How does *it* impinge on *me*? Textural perception always explores two other questions as well: How did it get that way? and What could I do with it?'

To touch is to perform, to trouble what it is that we do, but it also sets up a relation, a dialogue, with someone or something:

'to touch is always already to reach out, to fondle, to heft, to tap, or to enfold, and always also to understand other people or natural forces as having effectually done so before oneself, if only in the making of the textured object'.[3]

For Sedgwick, feeling can be grasped, in both senses of that word: physiologically and intellectually. Touch is thus something we can actively do. As such, it's connected to agency.

One of the materials I've worked with in workshops is clay, playdough, which appeals to me for its easy pliability. If writing were playdough, then... then we could see where that too-easy metaphor would take me by trying it with our hands; by getting little bits of green-red-yellow dough under our nails, as evidence of some material engagement; a sticky trace of a sticky process. Sara Ahmed prompts us, 'Think of a sticky object; what it picks up on its surface "shows" where it has traveled and what it has come into contact with'.[4]

All these exercises were about the capacity to receive, to let the body respond and self-organise, to imagine what's possible, to not-know and not-plan the experience in advance.

not planning

In 2018, I attended an artist workshop on 'not planning' at the Southbank Centre, funded by the Live Art Development Agency, and organised by the late Katherine Araniello (who harnessed humour in her engagements with disability, agency, and queerness), and Teresa Albor (who connects feminism and questions around ageism in her work). Nothing was planned, or hardly anything, and so I and the other artists and workshop leaders practised and performed our not-planning, spontaneously, irreverently, comfortably, for ourselves and for the public, as part of Unlimited, the Southbank's festival that celebrates the work of disabled artists. Before the workshop, my control freak heart couldn't quite imagine how such a weekend would 'work'. Well, it worked, precisely because we didn't work hard, and had permission not to.

The week following the workshop, I attended a voice seminar at the Lichtenberger® Institute in Germany on the concept of hysteresis. In physics, engineering, and biology, hysteresis describes a state of belatedness when something has an effect *after* we expect it, and possibly not where or how we expected it. It's an effect that retains potency long after the cause, to the extent that the cause becomes untraceable. We were asked to apply this concept of lag to singing and learning. Systems with hysteresis are nonlinear. You see where I'm going with this. For our voice to function healthily we cannot over-plan. Our nervous system reacts much better to stimuli that are playful, that induce rest rather than tension. The singing method I learned—which I now also consider a much broader pedagogical method—is about openness, patience, responsiveness, and resisting the urge to do something quickly or to reach a particular 'goal'.

folding

Artists can often become overly goal-oriented, and as such, like athletes, unstoppable, tireless, competitive. An effective piece of advice you might give the artist-as-athlete: become the best at resting.

In January of this year (2020), I went to a class at Movement Research intriguingly titled the Athletics of Intimacy, with the dancer K.J. Holmes. What was athletic about the class was the rigorous dedication to and discipline in letting go. A discipline of discovery. We became disciples of slowness.

To be moved and touched by strangers in dance demanded and bestowed trust. It felt gentle and soothing. My body became material. The class focused on improvised movement with K.J.'s prompts as invitations for internal physiological experiences rather than external athletic demonstrations.

These kinds of exercises and somatic experiments rubbed something in for me, namely that touch is knowledge—a non-linguistic form of knowing. It's a physiological toolkit that you can learn through your body.

One prompt was to allow our body parts to move like magnets. A play with resistance for which we occasionally turned up the volume. You move the other's body and let the other's body move you.

What are the support structures that allow you to rest? The

dancers became my support structure following a tiny panic earlier that day. Small panics can accumulate in your body. And the skin tightens and reddens; the lung collapses. One singing prompt given during a seminar at the Lichtenberger® Institute was to imagine the collapsing lung. A fellow singer panicked. At the time, I did not see the threat that the collapsing lung posed. I understand it now, but I also sense the promised liberation when we let systems collapse, when we surrender to an image or an idea that your body translates. A paradoxical freedom emerges when we let go of all that holding. That holding onto. Which gets under your skin.

'MAKE IT PITHY', proposed K.J. Holmes, in another prompt for movement.

The pith is the spongy white tissue of the orange, the bit under the skin. You have to get under the surface to be pithy, that is, to be concise in your expression. But pith is never pithy. An orange pith in its spread of interlocking parts of tissue is always excess. Surfeit. Abundance.

The theme of this movement class was wandering. I wanted to get lost in the wandering of my thoughts, let the wall and ground support my wandering. How could other bodies?

Or did I want to interrupt, intersect their path? Follow a path and then bend away from it before a possible collision. Like a tangent.

*

And, of course, despite or amidst all this magnificent malleability, you sometimes get stuck. You fall out of place. You find that things don't fit. Perhaps something is jabbing

out, is askew, is wobbly, slant, careening. And then you do
or don't realise that this is where the learning takes place.
When the foundations are a little shaky.

*

If I had to picture the lazy laboratory, my idea of
collaboration, as a room, it would look like this:

> My collaboration is an attic with a big window seat
> with seats for innumerable bodies and cushions
> with flowery patterns and bobbles and tassels. My
> collaboration is a room full of soft furnishings for
> lounging, for following the languorous trails of our
> thoughts, for fumbling, for movements without fear of
> edges. There will be no sharp edges. No cold corners
> for a corner can be turned. My collaboration is a
> miniature paper theatre with paper clothes and paper
> tea cups and paper beds and paper lanterns, easily made
> with our hands. In my collaboration there is never a
> shortage of paper. My collaboration is a disco ball full
> of language, a bathtub full of language, a fridge full of
> language, and my collaboration is a room that vibrates
> with the molecules that are ideas that are invisible, but
> perceptible, when you listen carefully, when you feel
> into your feet. My collaboration has underlying pipes
> that give it structure, history, a past. My collaboration
> is one gigantic veranda swing, always in motion, or
> always already containing the possibility of motion.
> This swing, which is my collaboration, is airy and
> the air on my skin is the same that blows through the
> window in the attic, through the chimney, the pipes,
> the paper... A polyphony of objects, of bodies, that loll
> around, with language.

<hr />

[1] Pauline Oliveros, *Sonic Meditations* (Baltimore, MD: Smith Publications, 1974), p. 19.

[2] Anni Albers, 'Tactile Sensibility', in *On Weaving* (Middletown/CT: Wesleyan University Press, 1965; repr., London: Studio Vista, 1974), p. 45.

[3] Eve Sedgwick, *Touching Feeling: Affect, Pedagogy, Performativity* (Durham and London: Duke University Press, 2003), pp. 13-14.

[4] Sara Ahmed, *Queer Phenomenology: Orientations, Objects, Others* (Durham and London: Duke University Press, 2006), p. 40.

Polyphony

This piece was commissioned by the German Translation Fund (Deutscher Übersetzerfund) in 2022 for the 'ABC of Translation' on *Babelwerk*, a new digital knowledge platform for literary translation.

'(All these phrases must be uttered simultaneously.)'

In 1914, an anonymous writer in the proto-Dada magazine
291 announced that

'In literature the idea [of simultaneism]
is expressed by the polyphony of simultaneous voices
    which say   different things.   Of course,
    printing is not   an adequate medium,   for succession
in this medium   is unavoidable and a phonograph is
        more   suitable.'[1]

(Simultaneism was a term   coined by the painters
        Robert and Sonia Delaunay,   describing a
    tendency   in painting   by which artists
        tried to capture   an aspirational polyphony of
    figures   and perspectives often by means of
        overlapping patches
        of vibrant *tones*.)

The Hellenistic Greek word πολυφωνία   from which we
    derive the word   polyphony,   actually means
        a 'variety of tones'.

Tone makes me think of texture,   the luminosity
            or   shades of a colour.
    Tone or tonus also means stretching.

We can stretch   polyphonous writing to mean a multiplicity
        of references or allusions in
    a text or artwork and   already we're in
            much more   interesting territory.

To write about or to enact?   Let's imagine you could
            gently put the needle down

on this inadequate page and see what it picks up.
Translation is—by definition—polyphonous
because it always contains   at least two
                            voices.

But it may not admit to it; or ignorance may sweep
        that reality   under the table.

Some translations, some texts,   are ardently homophonic
        They insist on   one voice
                (its resonant clarity, its authority).

                Polyphonous writing, for me, is something more
                    entangled, perhaps even messier.

        Polyphony does not impose a single truth. It weaves
            a thick textile of   de-centred declarations…

Literally,   many sounds or   many voices,
        a polyphonic musical composition
contains independent (or let's say *interdependent)* melodies
        rather than one   dominant voice with its
                subordinated accompaniment.

    In a conventional translational set-up,   the translator
plays the role of the accompanist,   feathering the chords
    mellifluously   in the background, providing some
        harmonic cushioning,   rather than being
    rhythmically or tonally differentiated
                in true contrapuntal fashion.
    If we think of polyphony in literature,   we usually think of
the multiplicity   of narrative voices (as Bakhtin famously does)
        or poetic speakers,   sometimes visually or
    conceptually overlapping or   fragmented.

(How many is many?)

Does material have a sound?   Well, yes.
Does it have many sounds?   & how
would you   translate them?

A polyphonous translation in sculpture or performance,
for example,   could mean that   many voices created it
   (practically)   or enabled it   (conceptually).

                    When text appears on a piece of fabric,
is that polyphony?   When a performance emerges from a
          process of reading-and-writing-through

                                   historical source texts,
is that polyphony?
          When an experimental essay consists largely or
                    even entirely of citations,
is that polyphony?

I'm deliberately stretching the metaphor here,
toning my critical muscles.

          You might disagree with me; that's great.
          You may join the polyphonic ensemble!

          Do you take your polyphonic translation
with milk and sugar,   as a throat-soothing Baroque fugue
   (I can already hear   the organ   leading me
                to a promised spiritual ecstasy!)
or do you like it a bit bitter,   a sort of Stravinsky-esque
   'swarm of spring pipes' or even a Cagean radio music,
                à la Imaginary Landscape No 4,
   where several performers switch between stations,
          tuning in and out   of snatches of dialogue,

music,   and crackling   white noise.
        Objects have voices, too—they are the chorus.

I think I first learnt about   polyphony   indirectly
   as a child   by listening to my grandmother's choir
at the Franciscan Church in Salzburg,   squeezed
     between   the intersecting pitches of high and low
   (I mean between the big coats,   on the hard bench,
in the choir loft) the mouthy organ behind us;
     filling my whole body with sound.

   (Maybe my first polyphonic piece was a mass by Schubert,
   itself a translation,   which sets text to music, excerpts it,
makes it conform   to musical rhythms and requirements.)

   When we work through other materials,
              we enrich   the textures,
          we make a weave, a web.
What does it mean to have all these voices around us?
     How do we learn to pay attention to them?

              A material might have   a hidden voice,
the voice of its making,   it   might tell its own stories,
   its own material biography,   where it's travelled, what
          or who it encountered   along the way.

          And what if
the source we're translating is already polyvocal?
              Then we multiply the voices!

A polyphonic translation might go to town   with all the
languages it can possibly accrue;   all the puns; all the
          translingual mayhem it can muster.

Wreak havoc on that stiff-upper-lip of language!
In polyphonic writing, form *is* the argument.

                            Some polyphonic texts
                    (or faux-polyphonic ones
like this one)
                    might even try to visually recreate a
        semblance of simultaneity   and rhythmic play, which
we could call a bit gimmicky.
                            A gimmick,
as Sianne Ngai notes is   'a labor-saving   device'; it
        is 'irritating yet strangely attractive'[2] perhaps because
'something   about the gimmick seems   too revealing
    of its aim: that of   giving its addressee what it says
                    it knows we want.'[3]

        But does polyphony give us what we want? Or
        translation? Don't we crave the ring of surety,   the pitch-
        perfect precision of a line, without the rumbling,
glitchy disturbance of the translation's underbelly!   Why
        would I want to hear several voices, when I could just
            hear the one true original?

I'd like to rewrite Sianne Ngai's definition of the gimmick
    by replacing the keyword 'gimmick' here with
'polyphonic translation',   let's see if it works:

        'Toggling between   wonder and trick,
        overvaluation   and correction,
        the [polyphonic translation] thus draws into   sharper
            relief   something about   the workings
                of   [writing],   just as [translation] reveals
                    [polyphony] as [a valid] aesthetic
                        form.' (p. 476)

                    Suddenly I have my argument for polyphonic
        writing   by means of a conceptual translation,
whereby I keep   the 'core'   but blasphemously
fill it with words   from a different realm.

Here's Adorno on the essay—I mean
on the polyphonic translation:

            'the [polyphonic translation's] innermost
                formal law is heresy.
        Through violations of the orthodoxy of thought,
                    something in the object becomes visible
                        which it is orthodoxy's
            secret and objective
aim to keep invisible.'[4]

            INTERJECTION: A writer has their own ever-evolving
            or returning repertoire of voices, different tones, affects,
            affectations, styles, genres, dialects, idiolects and all the
            rest of it.
            Interjection 2: So does the translator.
            Interjection 3: And the reader.
            Interjection 4: Or performer!
            Interjection 5: Oh happy co-mingling of voices!
            Interjection 6: None of them fixed.

Perhaps what draws me   to the concept of polyphony
        is that in all its potential chaos   and ambiguity
    and its overwhelming   sonic tapestry, it makes it nigh
impossible   to ignore that there's an awful lot going on.
        We may be confused, even   exasperated, but
        we recognise the labour,   the thinking.

In reality,   I find this polyphonic layout   very hard
   to read   myself.   I'm doing it
            against   my better judgment.

        Surrendering to the impossibility of real simultaneity
in writing,   let me return   once more   to the
omniscient narrator,   knowledge-wielding pen in tow,
      to say that   all this back and forth,   this
         shimmying which doesn't settle,   is just to say that
                translational making is deeply political.

When we let other voices into our 'own',   we undo
      that very possessive 'owning'   along the way.

---

[1] [Editorial], 'Simultaneism', *291*, 1 (March 1915), [p. 5].

[2] Sianne Ngai, *Theory of the Gimmick* (Harvard University Press, 2020), p. 1

[3] Sianne Ngai, 'Theory of the Gimmick', *Critical Inquiry 43* (Winter 2017), p. 475.

[4] Theodor Adorno, 'The Essay as Form', trans. by Shierry Weber, in *Notes to Literature*, vol. 1 (Columbia University Press, 1991), p. 23·

Cloudiness

Cloudiness is a video piece, commissioned by Anouk Luhn & Lena Hintze in 2021, for *The Game(s) of Translation* (https://lcb.de/digitalessay/the-games-of-translation/), in collaboration with LCB (Literarisches Colloquium Berlin) & TOLEDO, & the research group/ excellence cluster 'Temporal Communities' at the Freie Universität Berlin. The full video is available online and stills have been included here for reference and illustration. The video was also exhibited as part of the two-person show *There's no way I can know it, the object, or the body*, at Hoxton253, London, Feb-Mar 2022.

A quotidian scene: 'The curtain goes up on the beginning of Sunday. It is as if it were ordinary weather' (Gertrude Stein).[1]

I have long been fascinated by a citational use of theatre's conventions without enacting them.

I hold open my book with a slab of clay to copy a passage about the history of scaffolding.

Experimental translations make their scaffolding visible. To intentionally upset the truism of translational invisibility, the scaffold visualises a material process. This making-visible does not aim for a transparency of meaning. Experimental translations side with a certain cloudiness.

Lisa Robertson, poetry's soft architect, says 'The weather is a stretchy, elaborate, delicate trapeze, an abstract and intact conveyance.'[2] The weather allows for small talk in a foreign language, it gives us a rich vocabulary for affective states, for speculative observations.

I have tampered with the minimalist excavations of writing, but I lack the unflappability for such an assured disposition. I have a soft spot for the geometric drama of ornate artifice.

Sometimes a student writes 'History teaches us' or 'the scholarly literature agrees' and sometimes I let it go and sometimes I lecture them gently, but secretly envy their innocence to make clear propositional statements.

In an embrace of clouding the issue, I will speak near experimental translation today. In proximity to it and intimacy with it, rather than purely about it.

The Vietnamese-born filmmaker, writer, and academic Trinh T. Minh-ha explains her concept of 'speaking nearby':

'a speaking that does not objectify, does not point to an object as if it is distant from the speaking subject or absent from the speaking place. A speaking that reflects on itself and can come very close to a subject without, however, seizing or claiming it. A speaking in brief, whose closures are only moments of transition opening up to other possible moments of transition — these are forms of indirectness well understood by anyone in tune with poetic language. Every element constructed in a film refers to the world around it, while having at the same time a life of its own. [...] to speak nearby [...] is not just a technique or a statement to be made verbally. It is an attitude in life, a way of positioning oneself in relation to the world. Thus, the challenge is to materialize it in all aspects of the film— verbally, musically, visually.'[3]

More precisely, I want to think near the tactility of translation, its harbouring of touch. Its receptivity to other materials. What it picks up along the way.

When I think of language as material, let's say as viscous, gooey, slushy matter, I think of Mina Loy's 'mucous-membrane' and 'trickle of saliva'. I think of the abundant sensual furnishings of Lisa Robertson's poetry and prose.

I think of Sara Ahmed who reminds us that 'the word "furnish" is related to the word "perform" and thus relates to the very question of how things appear. Queer becomes a matter of how things appear, how they gather, how they perform, to create the edges of spaces and worlds.'[4] In translation, we feel the words' edges, listen for worlds.

My dog smacks his lips, stretches, yawns, asking me to enter his soporific, salivary language.

'[T]he haptic disrupts the prominence of vision as a metaphor for distant knowing as well the distance of critique, but it also calls for ethical questioning. What is caring touch in this context?'(María Puig de la Bellacasa)[5]

I think of poets and queer-feminist theorists because that's the lived, read, written experience I bring to bear on my thinking about translation across different media. Translation as my scaffold. Where the thinking of the building is on display. Besides, I always think about how things are made. What—from the process—is discarded to serve the finished product (if it is ever finished)–how do you cement the process into the work so it becomes integral to it?

When I was a child I had a ruler that allowed me to trace all kinds of shapes: hexagons, ellipses, triangles, and circles in different sizes. A plastic drawing aid, a geometric template for a collection of lines. I don't recall if this drawing aid was ever used in school or was just for playing but it taught me about the ease of the decal, the power of the proxy.

Is a translation always the retracing of shapes already carved, of thoughts already voiced, now tasked with a different sort of materialisation on a variable scale of proximity?

When I don't know how to continue I do one of two things: 1) I open a dictionary or look up the etymology of a word, its changing uses over time, its possible synonyms. This keeps me busy for a while. 2) I surround myself with books, with language as an ambient field floating in front of my eyes.

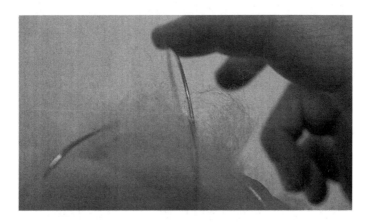

For Anni Albers:

'Material, that is to say unformed or unshaped matter [...] seems well fitted to become the training ground for invention and free speculation. . . .The crafts, understood as conventions of treating material, introduce ... traditions of operation which embody set laws. This may be helpful in one direction, as a frame for work. But these rules may also evoke a challenge. They are revocable, for they are set by man.

They may provoke us to test ourselves against them.'[6]

Lisa Robertson says in her '26 Theses on Craft', responding to Anni Albers:

> 'Materiality provides both freedom and limitation. [...] Material provides the limits by which the imagination might exercise its inventions. The abandonment of convention, however ardently desired, can never be entire because convention is itself a constellation of traces of historical relationships with matter. And yet BECAUSE WE CRAVE FREEDOM the differentiation must be made. Material will teach us where the new threshold between convention and freedom shall appear.'

Everything I've written or made over the last year somehow leads me to Albers' chapter on 'Tactile Sensibility'. I keep quoting it. It gives me guidance: 'Concrete substances and also colors per se, words, tones, volume, space, motion — these constitute raw material; and here we still have to add that to which our sense of touch responds — the surface quality of matter and its consistency and structure. The very fact that terms for these tactile experiences are missing is significant.' She asks us to pay attention to 'the surface appearance of material, such as grain, roughness or smoothness, dullness or gloss' and the 'inner structure' of a material or object: 'pliability, sponginess, brittleness, porousness'.

'The wire bends easily so we can shape it into any type of tree we want: the sort changed by constant wind, the weeping willow, the tree with branches that go up in all directions, the one ... we want' (Bruno Munari).[7]

But materiality is not just gentle, obedient, mannerly—material can be toxic, it can pinch, itch, it can ooze, it can go haywire.

To move and hold material is a translational act. It's a playful gesture. The late artist Elly Thomas called for 'an integration of the senses' through which 'the work' is 'continually … restructured', 'continually within process' which allows us to 'play with the life of the work.'[8]

As a translator you play with the life of the work. And like all play, all experiment, you're caked in uncertainty.

Uljana Wolf, the translingual poet and essayist I've most frequently translated, compares poetry to a game of hide-and-seek, with its 'hot and cold fumbling [...] in language'.[9]

Maybe translation is a matching game, a bit like rummy, where a meld can either be a set (also known as a book) or a run; so it's less about accuracy and more about the conceptual similarity.

A translation exists always in relation to another text. A non-translation is also always in a relationship with other texts but can more easily be in denial; it can hide its process of dialogue, it can pretend to believe in the fantasy of matchless authorship. Perhaps it's for that reason of undeniability, of blatant relationality, that translations aren't pretentious. They are, like the little magazines in which they usually first appear, a modest genre. A minor literature as Deleuze and Guattari call it.[10]

Wolf talks about Theresa Hak Kyung Cha 'deliberately construct[ing] [a] minority language with which the author interrogates cultural and aesthetic belonging and the political implications of listening.'

A translator—as a good reader, listener, writer—can highlight or dispel passages that have to do with power, with difference, with intimacy, aligning themselves with the work or bringing it into a different political and material context.

Playing with language can also mean resistance: Don Mee Choi's *Hardly War* uses translingual puns to attempt what she calls 'a new anti-colonial vocabulary of wound'.[11]

Sometimes we use language to interrogate certain ways of looking at objects and beings, or ways of being in our bodies, or for our bodies to be with others. We learn to care for the hidden, the small, the insignificant, the demoted, despised, marginalised, non-normative, things that don't fit, explode the template.

For Uljana Wolf, both experimental erasure poems and translations are about paying attention to what will disappear. In this way they are connected to memory, to visibility, to care. Translation in its intention to preserve, to prevent disappearance, commits that disappearing act.[12]

If translation is always residually monolingual and authorial (in the way it sets hierarchies and directions), it also froths these edges and is—inevitably, humbly—subsidiary. I mean this as a compliment.

In a recent interview in *The Capilano Review*, the dancer Dana Michel speaks about her process: 'When I'm doing research, I'm cloaked in an invisible velcro suit. Or a magnet suit. I'm in constant osmosis mode'.[13]

'I'm soaking everything up like a goddamm Christmas fruitcake. [...] I'm touching materials, talking, thinking, getting super swollen with all the information.' Translation as this fruitcake suit.

'I was most interested in how a body reacted in the time of performance after having worn this soaked fruitcake suit.'

LaTasha N. Nevada Diggs:

'I try on multiple languages like ribbons to better
understand the gaps in my lineage
and those histories indirectly related to me.'[14]

Anne Carson brings translation into not explicitly translational
projects. *Stacks*, a 2008 collaboration with choreographer
Jonah Bokaer and sculptor Peter Cole, sees performers dance
with cardboard boxes: they stack, restack, balance them on
their heads, move them, kick them over, let them fall, let them
tumble, drag them. At one point the cardboard boxes also
constitute the podium behind which Carson stands and from
which she recites her poem. The process the dancers enact is
translational, and translation, in turn, is a form of stacking.

The stacks provide at times a headrest, at other times they
weigh the body down, become unmonumental sculptures or
toys to be tossed around, or occasions for gymnastics, for a
duet, for what Uljana Wolf, in my translation, would call 'a
dabbling double', a 'twin language'.

Sawako Nakayasu, another translator and writer, brings
ants into the translation laboratory and onto the stage. In
her performance *Insect Country*, where the ants are co-
performers, Nakayasu asks what it means to be 'under the
tutelage of insects' and to have 'ant affinity'.

Nakayasu explains in an interview:

'I think that everything is connected by translation and by
a larger feeling of translation as movement and difference
and reiteration and new avenues towards thinking about
articulation. I could point to or talk about any single one

of my books through the lens of translation. The ant book, just as well, is a translation. It's just that in that book, everything is being translated through ants, but something is moving from one place to another. Usually when we translate, when we talk about literary translation, we're moving through one language to another. The wall that it passes is this linguistic difference, but that wall that it passes can be anything. It can be performative. It can be thematic or material or temporal. That's really interesting as a way to think about just being in the world.'

When I teach experimental translation, I ask students to read John Keene's essay 'Translating Poetry, Translating Blackness', getting them to think about how translation needs to be energised by the vital work in critical race studies, queer studies, disability studies, by small press publishing—work that teaches us how to destabilise what we know and how we've come to know it. But I also ask students to spend time with Keene's emotional outreach project, which consists of simple scores, reminiscent of Fluxus pieces, which are activated by readers. One of Keene's prompts I give to my students is to write out a beautiful line of poetry and leave it in public spaces.

Today I picked Yoko Ono's Cloud Piece.

Yoko Ono
Cloud Piece

Imagine the clouds dripping.
Dig a hole in your garden to
put them in.

1963 spring

An ordinary scene, an element of chance, a moment of transition, a simple playfulness spun into philosophy, into forms of connection, an attitude in life ... subtle translation of the everyday.

---

[1] Gertrude Stein, 'Am I to Go or I'll Say So: A Play in Places', in *Operas and Plays* [1932] (1998).

[2] Lisa Robertson, introduction to *The Weather* (New Star Books, 2001).

[3] Nancy N. Chen and Trinh T. Minh-ha, 'Speaking Nearby: A Conversation with Trinh T. Minh-ha', *Visual Anthropology Review*, 8.1 (Spring 1992), 82-91 (p. 87).

[4] Ahmed, *Queer Phenomenology*, p. 167.

[5] María Puig de la Bellacasa, *Matters of Care: Speculative Ethics in More than Human Worlds* (2017).

[6] Anni Albers, 'Work With Material' (1937).

[7] Bruno Munari, *Drawing a Tree*, trans. by Isobel Butters (Edizioni Corraini, 2019), p. 79.

[8] Elly Thomas, *Play and the Artist's Creative Process The Work of Philip Guston and Eduardo Paolozzi* (Routledge, 2019).

[9] Uljana Wolf, 'When You Can't Keep Your Cards Close to Your Chest', *Subsisters: Selected Poems*, trans. Sophie Seita (Belladonna, 2017).

[10] Gilles Deleuze and Felix Guattari, *Kafka: Toward a Minor Literature*, trans. by Dana B. Polan University of Minnesota Press, 1986), p. 17.

[11] Don Mee Choi in *Freily ausgefranst: Translingual Poetics*, ed. by Uljana Wolf and Christian Hawkey (Berlin: hochroth, 2019).

[12] A podcast conversation with Carolin Callies, 'Flausen mit Carolin Callies & ULjana Wolf' Literaturhaus Stuttgart, 14 April 2021. <https://podcasts.apple.com/de/podcast/flausen-mit-carolin-callies-uljana-wolf/id1520356250?i=1000517114630>

[13] Dana Michel, 'No Fixed Positions: A Dialogue on Yellow Towel with Dana Michel & Michael Nardone', *Capilano Review*, pp. 43-44 (Feb 2021), <https://thecapilanoreview.com/no-fixed-positions/>

[14] La Tasha N. Nevada Diggs, '56-26 Morton Street', in *Freily ausgefranst. Translingual Poetics*, ed. by Christian Hawkey and Uljana Wolf (Berlin: hochroth, 2019), p. 20.

Reading Fountain

This is a minimally edited script for a lecture performance
commissioned by the Royal Academy of Art for an event celebrating
Marcel Duchamp and Salvador Dalí in December 2017. It was
re-performed at the Center for Experimental Humanities, New
York University, in January 2018, at the invitation of Lori Cole and
Sukhdev Sandhu. Slides have been elided, except for the image on p.
127, titled *Five-Way Portrait of Sophie Seita (1917/2017)*.

[The set: a big armchair, a small table, a reading lamp. The artist enters dressed in a red sheer dressing gown. She sits down, and picks up her script, which has been carefully pasted into the folded board of Trivial Pursuit to make it look like a book; the title visible to the audience. She leans forward, head in hand, as if deep in thought, intently reading, holding herself and the text like a sculpture in stylised reading posture, in imitation of the genre of the 'reading woman' in Victorian paintings. She then looks up and begins to read to the audience, as if under candlelight:]

Part I: Reading Fountain

A definition:

A reading fountain: 'an ornamental structure in a pool or lake from which one or more jets of language are pumped

into the air'—'words that spurt or cascade'—'for decorative
or dramatic effects'—'a structure from which things flow'—
'a reservoir containing language that can be drawn off as
needed'—'a source of a desirable quality' as in—'a fountain
of wisdom'.

One of the most famous 'art works' of all time (tantalisingly
framed by quote marks) purports to be such a fine fixture of
porcelain elegance; a first-class intellectual thirst-quencher.

To 'read' *Fountain* again one hundred years after its first
sighting also invites a looking back before we can leap
ahead again. So let's turn our gaze towards the navel of its
conception. The 'original' *Fountain* was never exhibited. In
April 1917, it was submitted to the inaugural exhibition of the
Society of Independent Artists in New York, whose submission
policy decreed: No Jury! No Prizes! Not so. The piece, signed
and supposedly submitted by a certain 'R. Mutt,' was rejected.
The group around Marcel Duchamp was outraged and staged
a little riot in their magazine *The Blind Man*.

Replicas replicate but don't duplicate an experience. I'm
the editor of a facsimile reprint of this magazine which was
published by Ugly Duckling Presse. Holding a magazine in
your hands is a little more immediate than pawing at an
object behind glass. To mimic the original paper, size, and
design is to yearn to return to that past aura but this form of
copying also carries it into the present and makes it again an
object of our reading and care.

Little magazines like *The Blind Man* were and continue
to be sites of debate in which now-canonical works like
Fountain were first framed in an art-historical context; in
many cases, the editors and contributors self-consciously

created that context. The second issue of *The Blind Man* defended *Fountain*—notably with most of the page space given to female contributors. (Women are after all the real Judges of Allegory). In an anonymous editorial, titled 'The Richard Mutt Case' and sometimes wrongly attributed to Duchamp, Beatrice Wood, Duchamp's co-editor, upholds *Fountain* as more than 'plagiarism, a plain piece of plumbing.' Because R. Mutt 'CHOSE it', he made it a work of art: 'He took an ordinary article of life, placed it so that its useful significance disappeared under the new title and point of view—created a new thought for that object.'

What were *Fountain*'s new thoughts?

Selected for the occasion of a fictional name, an effort to marry the responsible submission, the attention to an object, to women climbing a staircase not meant for them and suddenly the pearls of pee bounced step by step entirely without jurisdiction and jury-approval so the executive committee was forced to identify the object itself as not physically manifest but displayed in camouflaged loops and ending in an apologetic letter. Aesthetic decisions are made in documentary fashion in romantic visions in immersion in defiance in venerated photographer's inventories, like the mutt-t-t-erings of symmetrical cameras all pointed at the mountain of secure support of slopes of gallery democracy. Wonderful, wonderful, they exclaimed! Another male artefact.

In her essay 'Buddha of the Bathroom', Louise Norton asserts that the answer to the question 'Is he serious or is he joking?' must come from the audience: 'It puts it rather up to you. [...] Perhaps he is both!' Perhaps he is both. Perhaps *I* am both. OK.

As Beatrice Wood had already insisted in the first issue of the magazine: 'Frankly I come to the [museum] to be amused. […] To laugh is very serious' indeed.

But first the public had to learn to appreciate new art 'like learning a new language', as the editors put it—meaning: a new conceptual vocabulary and a cultural openness to the unfamiliar. Dear decency! Dear craft! Dear genius! Adieu.

Alas, the public had 'spectacles on wholesome eyes', as the poet and artist Mina Loy lamented in her polemical essay 'In . . . Formation'. Drawn to 'information' rather than new art and writing which were still in the process of 'formation,' the public, for Loy, saw only 'something that has been seen before,' instead of 'seeing IT for the first time'.

Kathy Acker writes in her novel *Ripoff Red, Girl Detective*: 'Narratives you know are purely for shit. Here's the information go fuck yourself'. This is not a blasé shrug of dismissal, no concession to ideologically questionable laissez-faire intellectualism, but rather it's the provocation to take seriously the question of *what it is we are seeking to know and how we go about it*. That is what art and reading can give us. Ways of knowing that are different from the legible facts on our prescription drugs. As both Walter Benjamin and Bertolt Brecht realised, disruption is the medicine for drowsiness, while its habitual repetition may indeed induce it.

In other words, explication is the enemy of wonder, but sometimes its most political enabler. Put differently once more, illumination is the non-intrusive gentle guide to mark that manuscript, to enhance that passage. Perhaps out of devotion. Or a generous pedagogy.

oh sprawliness oh danger of the decorative oh museums

Even the shittiest primer on How to Write your First Novel will tell you: show, don't tell. Given that the critic's realm is the opposite of that—to tell (i.e. to read) the showing— there's a conundrum.

How can I both show and tell? Maybe by showing and telling two different, seemingly unrelated things, or two deceptively similar things? By showing the replica, but telling you about the original?

   Proximal objects invent the picturesque.

Much of history is hooked on the front cover when often what is most intriguing in an exhibition is the flip-side of what is shown.

The urinal's appeal was and continues to be its contextual, institutional, and even biographical framing. But this biographical framing is entirely retrospective. Duchamp's name did not appear anywhere in the magazine in association with *Fountain*, the identity of its true 'creator' was known only to a few friends, and there is still some scholarly debate as to whether *Fountain* was in fact a collaborative effort based on Duchamp's letter to his sister stating that a female friend had sent him the urinal as a sculptural gift. *Fountain* also shows similarities with another ready-made 'found' in the same year.

This female collaborator may have been the Baroness Elsa von Freytag-Loringhoven—an innovative émigré poet who became notorious in New York for her eccentric outfits: sometimes she wore a hat of vegetables she'd painted gold or a necklace made of a bird cage with a living canary in it.

[sings] ♫ *you're just an empty cage girl if you kill the bird* ♫

Was the Baroness erased from the story or did Duchamp simply conjure up a female alter ego? Both are convincing and apt for *Fountain*'s conceptual stunt of troubling traditional notions of genius.

✤

The nib of a fountain pen is its most iconic part. Thin, pointed, it draws ink, channels it through a small slit, spitting it onto a surface that receives it. Thanks to gravity and capillary caprice. The fountain pen contains an internal reservoir. Of liquid knowledge. It has no need for external supply.

An object is a material or metaphorical thing that can be watched and fondled and fiddled with. Presented to the mind. Outside myself.

Since *Fountain* was never exhibited, audiences would only have seen it as Alfred Stieglitz's photograph or as a replica decades later in museums like this one. As such a doubly reproducible and repurposed object, *Fountain*'s signature changes with use or non-use. Highly aestheticised, cleverly staged, and with his own signature all over it, Stieglitz photographed the urinal in front of Marsden Hartley's painting 'The Warriors'. Its porcelain cheeks glowing. Gloriously gay. From an object of routine inconspicuousness to an object of contemplation. It was made beautiful. The Fountain became a sacred object.

[The artist leaves the stage while a short segment of choreographer Anne Teresa De Keersmaeker's Fase, Four Movements to the Music of Steve Reich *(1982) begins to play in the background]*

Part II: Objects I Cannot Touch

[The artist enters wearing a turquoise blazer, a cheap vintage pipe in her mouth. The set: a chaise longue; leaning against it is an empty picture frame. A piece of heart-shaped soap is placed demonstrably on a pedestal which complements the scene. She picks up her script and reads:]

A lecture performance in two parts. Parts usually make up a whole. Or they may simply be temporal. One. Two. Like counting. A sequence with or without consequence.

The Blind Man's second issue contained another found object. This found object was language. Here's Mina Loy's conceptual collage poem: 'Will you bring a perfection, well bring a bottle—two perfections. [...] I used to kill myself with the syphon—You don't remember that ball. Well don't do that because I'm perfectly sober now. [...] I will give you some paper [...] keep silent.' 'She has a pencil in her hair' 'I want some tongue I will give you some' 'Censorship!' 'Well it is not dangerous at all' 'Well when he wants to imitate'...

Signing her piece 'Compiled by Mina Loy', Loy draws attention to her compositional method of *copying*. Loy 'collected' these snippets of conversations at The Blind Man's Ball, 'a new-fashioned hop, skip, and jump' for which 'Romantic rags [we]re requested.' One *could* imagine a twenty-first-century Blind Man's Ball, with audiences flaunting their fashionable irreverence. Though it would have to be injected with a revolutionary dose, as Anne Boyer promises when she notes: 'Dance music is closer to a true politics. Secret ballots and lots of talking and drone attacks are not a true politics, not like dance music. Those things are a pre- or post-politics. The body under dance music is the memory of the body under true politics, is the re-animated and revitalized polis. Under dance music there is [...] almost never a paucity of courage.'[1]

The Blind Man ended in a game of chance, of chess. A friendly competition between editors. Francis Picabia won and continued *391*. *The Blind Man* tipped its hat and printed the moves of the match in the new magazine *rongwrong*.

*

[Duchamp plays a melody on the piano. Swing or something. Or something that makes the toes tap.] [heckling: Distraction! Self-flagellation!]

Disputable 'out', ultimate 'off', interfering play with timid bias Always just births.

Everything top-secret.

Gaze: searchingly benign very well very well yes most probably gracious [sigh.] [Ommm][2]

*

How do we *read* Fountain? In French 'reading' means 'lecture'. In German 'Lektüre' means the process of reading and the object itself, the reading *matter*. Related to the Latin 'lego': I read, I gather, I take, I steal, I traverse, I pass through. To read out loud is to lecture, to instruct. What lessons do fountains teach us?

Roland Barthes writes in 'The Preparation of the Novel', in

Kate Briggs's translation: 'There is an age at which we teach what we know. Then comes another age at which we teach what we do not know; this is called research.'

That is also a way of reading.

Reading for form, for romance.
Etymologically reading is a guessing-game.
Followed by an impulse to advise.
Reading is unravelling. Of a dream, a riddle, perhaps.
It is a temple of enchantment, of refuge, of communal glue, of awakening, in which invisible angels gift the studious bookworms their wings of desire.[3]

If I perform the act of reading, am I not also reading?

I mean all you really want is to have your chin tickled like a little leopard that is housetrained. Most people live like that. Their lives are stable. But artists are obsessed with reading. A look that does not brush over but delves in, makes a world, sequentially, page by page.

The reader is the ultimate subject of provisional knowledge.

*

Duchamp was not the only one to submit a ready-made causing outrage at the Independents show: his co-editor Beatrice Wood exhibited a painting of a nude that replaced the traditional fig leaf with an actual bar of soap glued onto the canvas.

As commonly happens to the work of women artists, Wood's painting was read autobiographically with Wood being seen as the nude depicted, a fact she satirised in *The Blind Man*: 'And I was a piece of soap with nails in my back stuck on a canvas. A big flood came and swamped all the first floor [...] and I said to myself: those are the art-critics.'

Case in point: Unlike Duchamp, Wood is now more or less forgotten (although she did make an appearance in pop culture as the inspiration for the character of Rose in James Cameron's *Titanic*), and instead of choosing the life of a painter, she dedicated herself to ceramics, an art form much less highly regarded in twentieth-century criticism than the conceptual acrobatics of her male counterparts.

*

A portrait is a replica of one's identity. A portrait is a translation. Gertrude Stein, a contemporary of Duchamp, said this about portraits: 'The difference between thinking clearly and confusion is the same difference that there is between repetition and insistence. A great many think that they know repetition when they see or hear it but do they. A great many think that they know confusion when they know or see it or hear it, but do they. A thing that seems very clear, seems very clear but is it. A thing that seems to be exactly the same thing may seem to be a repetition but is it. All this can be very exciting, and it ha[s] a great deal to do with portrait writing.'

Fountain is also a portrait. Taken by Alfred Stieglitz.

*

To show a replica is to show an idea. A concept. A model. Which is malleable. When is a copy a commentary?

To interpret means to own. Temporarily. To acknowledge. To be responsible. And this may be a fabulous and flamboyant gesture of splashing, bubbling, and overflowing possibility.

A 'copy', as Bruno Latour and Adam Lowe point out, is a sibling of 'copious': 'and thus designates a source of abundance. A copy, then, is simply a proof of fecundity.' 'One will never see the original, [...] but only several premieres and several [...] versions with endless glosses and variations.' One performance, or one publication, becomes part of the work's 'ongoing biography'.

But what if the work is so transformed to only bear the trace of resemblance, or, in some cases, only reveals its trace in language—if I tell you so. If I made it up.

'To photograph is to appropriate the thing photographed. It means putting oneself into a certain relation to the world that feels like knowledge—and, therefore, like power.' (Susan Sontag)

What does it mean to appropriate a copy (or a copy of a copy)? Or maybe the more interesting question would be: What does it mean to take the copy seriously? To insist on it. To follow its invitation to play and replay. To reuse a particular form or practice. This is not a facile question but one at whose intersections of race, gender, sexuality, and class the fountain gains its curvature; without which no water would fly or plunge. The form itself does not speak clearly. What would the conditions have to be today for a fountain to be rejected? And why would we even seek that frisson of the negative, of the radical break?

*

This is how we read the visual:

The transient subject is caught in a grid of abstraction, the surrounding elements suitably archetypal to act as visual symbols, metaphoric extensions, with the body being read itself as a language. A commentary on language, then, on gestures of reaching, and the unavoidable particularity of the body. A geometrical playground with invisible barriers—a matrix, within which the dancer moves with the grace of a peculiar provisionality.

When Maya Deren gazes at her double in her surrealist film *Meshes of the Afternoon*, the double performs movements the on-looking Maya has already performed, except in one scene she's failing to run up the stairs, held back by a storm blowing from paradise. The staircase is rocking. The house may collapse. Who is copying who in this sequence, this dream?

From Bernadette Mayer's *Utopia*:

'I hope the future was fine and you enjoyed being in it with us, we tried to make you comfortable and clear. Not everything's been attended to yet though, but when you know more, and I do, then tell me more about the naïve and serious and perfect and telltale and generous and satiric things, and we will have together an adjectival future which already lives in our kitchens and in the windows of our clear panes, if we have kitchens and if we have windows to see and cook from to mitigate our food by the visions of others whom we all love and with whom we will all easily eat in a big generous gratuitous free peace.'

＊

Things usually flow because one thing is higher than the other. The greater the height, the greater the gushing, the pressure.

In the Trevi Fountain in Rome, the water—I mean language—churns and tumbles and flushes to add movement and drama. It is widely acknowledged that *this* altered the appearance, function, and intent of fountains: a watershed for our artistic futures.

Filling just above the mouths, the spouts, of the canons. Ready?

＊

Enter a French artist F dressed as a judge. Enter a German spy D dressed as a 1980s TV show host.

What are these women's voices
And moose
Monsieur F did you hear that
F: Many things that were said to me I didn't understand. They didn't seem to me to be quite French. / I didn't deem them to be quite French. / I didn't seem to be quite French.
D: They were masked.
F: When they raided the village. And always they take the women with them. And honey.
D: She sings so beautifully. Why don't you listen come on listen can't you hear
F: This name I know! This title
D: Do they have enough dots spots enough colour for your taste? / Are they dotted enough are they coloured enough? The parts do they

and still. / continuing still. / still continues. better. more tender(ly) / gentler. white and many many more. and many many many they are not one if it was one that would be better. and whiter. but it pitches/raises/institutes and yanks itself/ wrests itself up to a landing/touchdown yes almost unwatched/ quite unobserved/under the radar just just without any truly without any. in observance one can regard this provisional(ly). floating. thinks yes expedient / conveniently usable and mixes/ mingles (itself) quite queerly/peculiar. modest/simple and mixed you hold it in parts/portions because as you name it it is parts/ portions even if you think Unity it isn't you're holding the hip aren't you there you go a part.[4]

'Everything contradicts my perception.'

[The artist sits down on the chaise longue, next to the empty picture frame, and blindfolds herself with a silk shawl, she looks straight at the screen, which now plays her video Objects I Cannot Touch (2014).*]*

---

[1] Anne Boyer, *My Common Heart*, p. 35.

[2] This short sequence is adapted from Sophie Seita's '3,4', published in *Fantasias in Counting* (BlazeVOX, 2014).

[3] In preparation for this lecture performance, I posted on Facebook asking friends to send me some of their favourite scenes of reading (especially women reading) in films and books. My friend Corina Copp suggested Wim Wenders's *Wings of Desire*.

[4] This whole section is also taken from 3,4 published in *Fantasias in Counting* (BlazeVOX, 2014).

POETRY'S PHANTOM LIMBS

Commissioned for the exhibition *FIGURE/S: Drawing after Bellmer* (London, Drawing Room, 2021) and published in an anthology of the same name by MA BIBLIOTHÈQUE (2021), edited by Kate Macfarlane, Michael Newman, Sharon Kivland and Louis Mason.

*

You're told that your sources were sublime but they expected greater solemnity. Well, they lack flaming buoyancy, I say, they lack flair. I parade the extravagant figures. Do you recognise this figure of speech? I don't. Yet another rhetorician is putting poetic simplicity before politics; or 'rules of the genre' before mannerist triflings—they matter. I want the trifles. The truffles. Pure pathos. As if that were possible. Give me the hidden figures then. Fine, she says, throw in the towel for an ethos of uncertainty that I can easily do without. I'm very precise. The fact remains that—

I. I Need to Figure it Out

Figuring stuff out is poetic business. As a poet, I trade in that process. I profess it.

Already, I feel uneasy, in the declarative. Something's a little off. Something's gone missing. Somewhere along the line I stopped writing poetry. And yet the self-identification slipped off the tongue so easily. And yet I can still feel Poetry pulsing, sometimes sharply, sometimes gnawingly, in the pit of my stomach, like intense infatuation or a dull ache, making itself known.

A phantom limb describes the physiological awareness when, say, a lost or amputated body part still releases sensations of pain, pleasure, weight, or shape, *as if* the limb was still there.

This *as if* is an effective fiction, an *effiction*, as Peter Szendy argues in *Phantom Limbs: On Musical Bodies*, a book dedicated to the very real effects of fictional and sonorous bodies, their substitutability, their various prostheses.

The poet's prostheses are figures of speech.

Effictio is one such rhetorical figure, a depiction of a body through language, sometimes with forensic detail, a scanning from head to toe. This literary word-portrait fashions something, represents something, gives it shape.

So, we, phantom-poets, we workers-in-language, we embroider, we clothe in finest eloquence and decorative panache, we powder and puff; we offer precious ornaments and exacting designs; and in this way, in this way of making-body, we have made language desirable.

That is the phantom pleasure of poetry.

But a phantom is also the imprint left by ideas and words. A decal. You can trace the line of thought but its opacity, its surface, won't quite give. Something feels as if it's there and the next moment you doubt its existence. In this sense, the phantom is connected to the woolly tangibility of memory. The work of the phantom, which is also the work *on* the phantom, its *figuring-out*, represents the process of writing and learning. How we make sense and give shape to what we know. (I need to figure it out, my refrain, I refrain.)

But where does that *out* lead us? When someone is out, they're not at home. When something's out, we're at the end. We fill out the form, the blanks, which are provided for us, by lines. To 'figure it out' means to begin to understand. That movement toward completion is only ever approximate. I'm intrigued by this half-knowledge, a knowledge that's provisional, incomplete. To figure it out is the gesture of the reader. We learn to decipher without solving the puzzle.

Whenever I want to figure something out, I go to a dictionary. I learn that 'prosthetic' can also mean a letter or syllable attached to the beginning of a word, such as Spanish *escuela* derived from Latin *scola*, school.

In school, we figure things out through repetition. We repeat verb endings or the declensions of nouns in Latin, which I used to memorise diligently, even pleasurably.

	Singular / Plural
Nominative	Corpus / Corpora
Vocative	Corpus / Corpora
Accusative	Corpus / Corpora
Genitive	Corporis / Corporum
Dative	Corpori / Corporibus
Ablative	Corpore / Corporibus

Latin, perhaps because of the declensions, was all about figuring out what the hell was going on, who did what to whom, or when something was (or is or will be?) happening to an object directly (accusative) or indirectly (ablative).

In Latin, the body, the corpus, becomes grammatically deformed. Something is being done to the noun every time it speaks.

Such contortion needs practice, a little musical salve. When you learn a foreign language, you learn it like a tune. You chirp the irregular verbs, you make grammar rhythmically bendable. Which is an aid to memory.

To serve their mnemonic purpose, several figures of speech work through sound and repetition, like alliteration, anaphora, assonance, or onomatopoeia. Others work through juxtaposition, or we could say the imbrication, of simultaneous meanings: irony, metaphor, simile, paradox. Some break wholes, break bodies, to stand in, to substitute; they make us partial, fragmentary, like synecdoche and metonymy. Some are figures of gymnastics, like puns and anagrams; they deliberately misread and twist and re-arrange letters or words. And in this re-arrangement to form new words—a repetition of material which is effectively invisible—the pun and anagram have created a phantom.

Similar to phantom limbs, some metaphors, which are an implied resemblance, are derived from the human body and then often extended to inanimate objects. So the eye of a needle, the bowels of the earth, and the mouth of a river, congregate into a poetic anatomy, are drawn into perspective through their dismemberment, so we can picture them. There is a violence in this dismemberment. Metaphors and metonyms relating to the body are problematically entwined with theories of the body. The body as an idealised whole which, when broken, is usually written as in need of repair or as a spectacle. There can be a violence or tenderness in imagining and describing the body.[1]

Importantly, figures of speech are also connected more directly to the body, through gesture. Orators and rhetoricians, such as Quintillian or Cicero, used to orchestrate their hands to make a point: to punctuate, underline, and illustrate. Hand gestures and their angular relationship to the body were and are a part of speech, a language of the body (sermo corporis). For Kathy Acker, in turn, a language of the body emerges from a rejection of ordinary language, and is like body-building 'always working around failure'.

Which makes me think of how language draws a line between what's there and what's imagined, between what's yours and what's borrowed, or how it buoyantly fails to do so. 'Draw a line', as an imperative, can be instrumental for your thinking, your body. It can also be instrumentalised. The pencil is an instrument. So is the hand. 'My body is an extension of my body' (Barbara Browning).

Lines lines lines where's the line in this ruminating longevity?

Okay, let's toe the line of the essay form.

Sometimes what's *not* there can be more present than what is.

You can feel the body without the body. Or poetry without the poetry. All paradoxes vanish.

To repeat, to clarify, to undo ambiguity, against my poetic desire. I've thrown in two meanings of poetry's 'phantom limbs' here: Poetry as my phantom limb and Poetry's own generically integral phantoms, through which it always acts, which it has by definition, by way of its artifice, its being made. I'm not sure if I've convinced you, or myself, of this thought experiment. I'm not sure if I've kept these two meanings sufficiently separate.

In a play, I might say: A figure appears at the corner of the stage as if treading on thin ice.

II. Learning to Play

In December 2019, I was given the London studio of an artist I met in New York a few months earlier. It was the first time I really had a studio and for the first time I felt what some writers might feel when they sit in front of a blank screen, a blank page, but which I rarely feel because I always surround myself with words, which guarantees that I never feel alone. Now I had a blank space. So much room to move around in, so much to fill *out*, so much possibility; and no words. I didn't know where to start. I set myself the goal of working on a new performance and video, specifically on the costumes and movement. I spent one morning dancing around, gathering ideas for gestures, structures, lines of direction. That was 'productive'. One afternoon, I bought some bronze wire (bronze for third place—the piece I was working on is partially about competition), and two gloopy paints that resemble nail varnish but when dried reveal a texture that looks like cells quivering; like a leaf cut open. I wanted the viscerality of paint. I desired the messiness of a painter. I made ambitious plans to make a mask and a costume with that paint, even to destroy and appropriate an old canvas in our flat. My partner counselled wisely that I could just buy a fresh blank canvas. I ended up making her a Christmas card with the visceral paint instead.

During these musings, I could not help but think about Frank O'Hara's 'Why I Am Not a Painter'. It's a poem about process. In it, O'Hara describes visiting the studio of his friend, the painter Mike Goldberg. The painter in the poem paints sardines, the poem feigns surprise: 'there's sardines in it' as if sardines didn't belong in a painting. Later, the depiction of the sardines disappears, and what's left is something else without apparent traces leading back to the beginning. Later, the poet writes a poem 'about' orange where the word doesn't appear. He calls it *Oranges*. Later, in the artist's exhibition, all remnants of the process have disappeared in the paint; what's left is the title. The painting is called *Sardines*.

What lesson does that poem (or painting) teach us about the process of making? About reading and intention? The poem shows us the many ways we could approach any text or work of art: we could read the work formally and speculate why on earth an abstract painting (or even a figurative painting) is called 'Sardines' when nothing resembling a sardine is visible. We learn about seeing and not seeing and that paintings and poems can see things that the reader can't and *vice versa*. Perhaps we would try to trace the lines; remind ourselves what a sardine looks like. But soon we would find ourselves in the realm of metaphor. We might picture sardines squashed together in tins. Perhaps, we would then surmise, the painting metaphorises the experience of squashedness, and the work could be an allegory of human and/or animal curtailment in our tin-can world, or perhaps the titular sardines are the sardines found on the streets of Portugal and the work becomes a joyous celebration of a holiday or childhood memory.

In many ways, the poem is like the chess-playing automaton that Benjamin discusses in *Theses on the Philosophy of History*, supposedly pulling the strings, sharing a secret with us. Secrets are the sap of biography. Revealing secrets makes biographical readings juicy. The critic or audience as investigator or gossipy neighbour. Alternatively, the poem says: OK, all you critics can keep looking at sardines or oranges as much as you like but you will not know the 'true' meaning behind the work; in other words, the work is a mystery; or rather: the work's meaning lies with you, not with the maker.

For me, the poem contains all these routes of reading, and also suggests a healthy casualness. So what if I want to call my work *The Intrusion of the Blue Jelly Globes* or *Bending to Banal Blurriness* (the first phrase I got from words I spotted on my tiny airplane screen and the printed matter peeking out from the seat pocket, the second after looking at someone else's screen trying to decipher the shapes)?

What a title like *Sardines* or *Oranges* also asks us to do is to imagine a link, a leap. To associate a with b. To ask: what do 'oranges' or 'sardines' make me think of? And also: what in the text resonates with my association? What supports it and what contradicts it? Is what I see the same as what I take a word to mean? It all comes back to how you make something juicy, or chewy.

In my 'notes to myself' after a performance in 2018, I wrote: spend a day with a prop.

The last day at the holiday studio I asked the bronze wire to give me some ideas. I wrapped it around my body. I danced with it. I made it my mascot. I pressed it into my cheeks, made it dent my lips, frame my eyes, pull up my chin. I intended it to be a playful, gentle exercise, but the wire desired otherwise. It pricked me. I realised that any sort of documentation of this crossing of metal and flesh would immediately exceed my own planned interpretations. I wondered how I would read it if I could feign ignorance of myself. I thought of Oskar Schlemmer's *Drahtfigur* (Wire-Figure) in his geometrical *Triadic Ballet*. Wire is constriction. Is wire always cold? Is wire in relation to a face always a muzzle?

Something is tingling, tickling, me, as I type (think?) this sentence, before I can tell whether it's there or not.

I've run out of words.

What is poetry without its figures, its phantoms?

What if we give poetry some physiotherapy to make the phantoms disappear?

Without limbs, without phantoms, poetry hovers,
frictionless, above the world and its tasteless realities,
peering aimlessly into the drought-cracks of prose.

---

[1] I'm thinking of the excellent collection *Bodies in Commotion: Disability and Performance*, edited by Carrie Sandahl and Philip Auslander. Pages 2-4, 36, 138-139 are just a few instances where the idea of the disabled body as in need of cure or as an object of spectacle is refuted. See also 'Breaking the Boundaries of the Broken Body' by Margrit Shildrick, Janet Price; and Tom Shakespeare, 'Culture Representation of Disabled People: Dustbins for Disavowal? (1994).

Thinking the Body Outwards

Originally commissioned by and published in *Flesh Arranges Itself Differently* (The Roberts Institute of Art and The Hunterian, University of Glasgow, 2022). The original title was 'Fig. 3.2: An Anatomical Lecture, or, Thinking the Body Outwards' in reference to two anatomical drawings included in the exhibition.

Do we always begin from the fingers outwards? Imagine where they point, what they cannot reach or hold or pierce? All descriptions ride this imaginary Möbius strip.

Your preference might be for an object that has purpose, is easy to carry. Something light, a whiff of a thing. But the object I'm asking you to picture is lumpy, ill-defined. It clings to the surface like fluff to plastic. Indistinguishable matter.

It's desperate to appear plummy, like cheeks which an annoying uncle squeezes until they hurt. The object wants to become one with the atmosphere, a little shivering molecule, bobbing along to the room's rhythm. It's hard to follow the contours of the material without getting it all mixed up with the sensation.

*

The lecturer points, whacking you with the empiricist stick. Stabbing an open wound. We could call this a 'rational' scholarly description ('amenable to observations and experiment'), a proper enlightenment gesture, or more metaphorically: an anatomy of criticism, where everything becomes a subject for reading. An object of our perception.

I want you to follow the fleshiness. Where does it lead you?

We might remark casually that the object is 'well furnished with flesh; fat, plump.' We might make 'fleshy' our style.

Ben Johnson concurs: 'It is a fleshy style, when there is much Periphrases, and circuit of words; and when with more then enough, it growes fat and corpulent.'[1]

Mei-Mei Berssenbrugge adds: 'It's a style of accumulating materials that does not become a solid thing, anymore.'[2]

I surrender to this fleshiness and am simultaneously deterred by it. There is no formula for the body's legibility. When the anatomist attempts to numerically impose order, the écorché figure laughs heartily.

Flesh is a framework. All scenes of making can be exposed.

The unclothed body functions much like a window. It is not made for readers. Readers prefer the voluminosity of layers. Curtains. Collars and cuffs. Bow ties. Wigs. They rummage in their dusty folds.

*

Let's imagine you have the same lecturer alongside their student standing by the operating table watching the proceedings. One measures the viscosity, or velocity, or maybe even the gravity, the other notices the invisibility of the heart; the shine of the fascia reflecting the sun. Neither understand how to wind pleasurable knowledge into the stable and fixed stature of 'the body'. They don't need to.

Is there anything that can be known with certainty? Does a thought cause the flick of the wrist or is the hand slamming the door on the mind?

We could well imagine a different arrangement of our body. Could my mind sit on my kneecap? Could it pinch my bum cheek? Squeeze out from under my armpits? Itch or rub like a piece of clothing that's a bit too tight or maybe it floats loosely around my flesh, sometimes touching my calves as

I shimmy and swirl about. I extend my arm. I roll onto one side. How can I make this very simple?

Let me put my Spinozist t-shirt on.[3] What can the body do? Bodies, for Spinoza, are defined by what they come into contact with (and some of these objects, as Sara Ahmed argues, are simply not within our reach).[4] If we do not yet know how far or in what way the body's power extends, why impose limits on it? How would I move or write without knowing what this body can do? Abstractions also conjure a body, a scene, an object, a room, beyond the 'correct', the 'normal', the 'standard'. And even further: 'What might we forfeit by troubling this idea of a body as 'mine'?' (Astrida Neimanis, *Bodies of Water*). Approximating something more distributed, relational, we might ponder, what would this body look like? How light or heavy or bulbous or squishy would it be? How would it move? Swollenly. Ballooningly. '[A]nyone's face made bulbous in the cave of a silver spoon.' (Kat Addis, *Space Parsley*). Hogarth would probably find this 'too bulging, or too tapering', 'too bold', not precise enough for his serpentine 'line of beauty'. (A mildly scoliotic spine, like mine, twists slightly to one side, making a curved line, like an S.) But what is precision in description? The precise way to represent the pain under my shoulder would be by means of an abstract orange-pink platonic solid poking out at the viewer. It would be excessively (or obsessively) dotted and have prick-marks, or maybe reveal the somewhat rough surface of a gessoed wooden panel, cut to size, with the edges un-sanded.

Eleni Stecopoulos writes: 'My metaphors did not cause my symptoms; my symptoms did not provoke my metaphors. But in their uncanniness they signified the affinity, the synchronicity of all interpretive work in my life during this time. They were part of the same pattern [...] Illness made visceral that the world did not move by cause and effect, but [...] by correspondences.'[5]

*

Categories and inventories and indices start to tremble and quiver, and in their quivering create a delightful blur, testing your eyesight, the objects are still there, outside of periods, beyond the classifications of knowledge into 'disciplines', no disciplining of the flesh,[6] and in this sweet spot they assemble and convene, away from the anatomist's hall, where they'd be splayed out on the dissecting table for everyone to see; you try to recognise them; and then the line appears again, wobblier this time; and you make out a face, briefly, it is the face of your beloved; you look at her, and aim for the words to pop out like bubbles to fizz into a poem, but instead they dissipate, and you curse the tongue, the lip, the jaw: 'Language, you terrible surrounder / Of everything, what is the good / Of me isolating my few words / In a certain order to send them / Out in a suicide torpedo to hit? / I ride it. I will never know.' (W.S. Graham 'Implements in their Places')

Anatomy is too skimpy a technique. In my stretchy shirt, I begin to play with rubber surfaces, with slopes, I embody being unfit in this environment. I clamber. I tumble. I do not know the right way for body and object and floor and fabric to interact.

I 'have' a feeling. It's totally conditional on the context. On this almost dancerly pose. Seemingly unconnected shapes bubble up and I brush them into a little pile for analysis. We both watch as I form the feeling into matter.

I make out another figure. It is arresting. The arms of the fabric are stretched out like a windswept scarecrow or a parent. I would like to speak to the figure; draw geometric circles, like cloudy speech bubbles. It smacks me in the face; I'm there for it. I will it to happen. I'm wide awake.

Something brushes my shoulder that feels like styrofoam. Or maybe sawdust. My fingers reach for it.

---

[1] B. Jonson, *Timber; or, Discoveries*, 2072 in Wks. (1640) III, qtd. in OED.

[2] Mei-Mei Berssenbrugge, 'Permanent Home', in *I Love Artists* (University of California Press, 2006).

[3] See: Léopold Lambert and Minh-Ha T. Pham, 'Spinoza in a T-Shirt', *New Inquiry* (1 July 2015).

[4] 'If we are shaped by "what" we come into contact with, then we are also shaped by what we inherit, which delimits the objects that we might come into contact with.' Sara Ahmed, *Queer Phenomenology*, p. 124. See also Merleau-Ponty, *Phenomenology of Perception* p. 31, regarding our attention's 'elucidation of the object' by 'placing it there', thus making it legible.

[5] Eleni Stecopoulos, *Visceral Poetics* (ON: Contemporary Practice, 2016).

[6] Alexander G. Weheliye's *Habeas Viscus: Racializing Assemblages, Biopolitics, and Black Feminist Theories of the Human* (Duke University Press, 2014) shows how race disciplines bodies into human, non-human, or 'not-quite-human'. Bodies are subjected to a 'hieroglyphics of the flesh' in Hortense Spillers' formulation, stripped of gender and humanity and are thus made excessively visible and legible, but flesh as a category also offers a 'relational vestibule to alternate ways of being' (p. 44).

Touching Things to Give them Names
(An Epilogue)

'to recognise that we touch one another in language'
—bell hooks, *Teaching to Transgress*

'collecting is only one process of renewal; other
processes are the painting of objects, the cutting out
of figures, the application of decals—the whole range
of childlike modes of acquisition, from touching
things to giving them names.'
—Walter Benjamin, 'Unpacking My Library'

My skin chafes from rubbing—reacting with my hand's heat.
I peel off a thin layer. A stick-on tattoo of a wonky butterfly.
A faded decal.

A decal is a transfer.

The word 'decal' is a shortened form of the French
décalcomanie, which comes from décalquer 'to transfer a
tracing'.[1] *Décalcomanie* is literally a transfer-mania, a fever
for repeated copying—a kind of Derridean *mal d'ecal*?

More specifically, decalcomania describes the process of
adding paint to one side of a sheet of paper, glass, or canvas
and pressing the two sides together, letting them rub against
one another, leaving an imprint. From the nineteenth
century onwards, many artists, particularly the surrealists,
became fascinated by the accidental forms that emerged
through this practice of tactile, imprecise copying with
unpredictable outcomes. For me, the decal, then, is both a
real process for making new work out of existing material
and a metaphor for the type of lesson I want from art.

*

163

When I was an undergraduate student, I wrote something like 20 pages of what I hoped would become a novella about a woman called Eleanor, in love with another woman (a dancer) in Spain. Eleanor was an aggregate of my sloppy reading of Hélène Cixous' and Melanie Klein's feminist psychoanalytic theories and a thinly veiled roman-à-clef. It involved some intricacies and intergenerational trauma around mothers and secrets, and diaries and dreams. I was enamoured, for a while, with the idea of it, and with Eleanor. I never finished the novel. A plot does not intrigue me enough to keep me going. I do not want to follow a character around and I do not care enough about what might happen to her. At some point, the work broke into poetry, at other points it became a dramatised Beckettian dialogue between Eleanor and her psychoanalyst. What I did do, however, was later re-use that conversation for a magazine I edited. I replaced the psychoanalyst with an unnamed interviewer and the name 'Eleanor' with the name of one of our contributors, Birte Endrejat, a conceptual artist from Berlin.

BIRTE *How do I remember what I have learned?*
TEXT *How could you not?*
BIRTE *But does it all make sense?*
TEXT *The one whole almond in the pudding. [Titters.]*
BIRTE *Sorry? Sorry.*

I often re-use language. My own and other people's. I take words and press their two sides together; I let language make blurry butterflies on my skin. Once upon a time I felt some embarrassment about that recycling, because of the unspoken assumption that to re-use material is somehow cheating. It's as if I'd run out of ideas. But then I remind myself:

'You create identity, you're not given identity per se. What became more interesting to me wasn't the I, it was text because it's texts that create the identity.' (Kathy Acker)

Ditto: 'you make the I and what makes the I are texts.'[2]

TEXTS MAKE ME.

Is this my statement for art making, my acknowledgement of a serious and playful engagement with texts?

My friend Kat, in turn, assures me that reusing my own words or work in different contexts just shows that my thinking hasn't finished. Things are still active, provisional.

*

I once attended a lecture 'On Marx' by the German literary scholar Hans Ulrich Gumbrecht. What was striking about the lecture which was supposedly about *ideas* ('What's left of Marx?') was its insistent biographical tilt. Gumbrecht talked mostly about Marx as a child and student, framed by Freudian questions such as: 'what was the driving force behind Marx? What were his motivations?'

I learned two things:

1. Although Marx was a brilliant student, he often did not achieve what he wanted and therefore felt undervalued. This made him even more insistent on a 'justice' of value which, according to Gumbrecht, explains all of Marx's work. I liked the image of Marx as a sulking teenager. I liked the suggestion that abstract ideas aren't untethered from personal experience. In fact, big ideas are often rooted in small disappointments or things not going exactly the way we had planned.

2. Gumbrecht admitted proudly that throughout his career he has only had one great idea ('presence') and has been writing variations of that idea ever since.

Both appealed to me a great deal as an approach to learning and writing.

*

bell hooks, teacher of liberatory pedagogy, writes wisely in *Teaching to Transgress:* 'I came to theory because I was hurting [...]. I saw in theory then a location for healing.' I am deeply moved by this comment as it resonates with my own experience of turning to texts, to theory, to make sense of the world or rather: to feel held in its frequent not-making-sense.

And yet, hooks also cautions us: 'Theory is not inherently healing, liberatory, or revolutionary. It fulfills this function only when we ask that it do so and direct our theorizing towards this end.'

What is this 'toward'? How do we direct Theory? What do we ask of her?[3]

*

I've been thinking about this book as a *kind of* bibliophilic memoir. Admittedly, the word 'memoir' is immediately setting off my own alarm bells. I start visualising Super 8 footage of a curly-haired kid with her head in the books—pass!

I wouldn't be a good student of Kathy Acker's and Christine Brooke-Rose's experimental autobiographical writing if I could simply drop my suspicion. But was I drawn to Brooke-Rose and Acker because I was already suspicious of the sincerity of the 'I', or was I *taught* to be suspicious of it? And did reading these two figures who questioned traditional 'portrait[s] of an eye' (Acker) only consolidate my literary taste?

There's something both edifying and embarrassing about Brooke-Rose's insistent discomfort with memoir, with readerly ease. Repeatedly she informs her readers that she has been misunderstood, neglected, just because her work is difficult. Plagued with 'biofatigue' (her term for being fatigued with biography), Brooke-Rose moans: 'experimenters like me are doomed to die and be forgotten'.[4] Her fear of 'escaping' the canon, which also tormented *Textermination*'s Mira Enketei, permeates her criticism and fiction. Brooke-Rose knows that if you 'do something very difficult', there is a danger that 'nobody notices'.[5] *Remake*, Brooke-Rose's experimental memoir, is peppered with commentary about her dislike of her own chosen genre, suggesting the underlying fear: is *Remake* perhaps 'only' an autobiography with some theoretical cladding? Brooke-Rose is concerned about a potential lack of intellectual weight. I sympathise. Perhaps too much. Have I adopted her obsession?

William Empson comforts me: 'the mere number of possible interpretations is amusingly too great'.[6]

It's perhaps not an accident that my book evolved only when I had properly left my own 'schooling' and was rethinking who I was, as an artist, a teacher, a person. I also needed to work something out, like Suzanne Cusick: 'I needed to work it out. I needed to understand what relationship, if any, I could suppose to exist between my being a lesbian and my being a musician, a musicologist.'[7] The pieces in this book came to me at a time when I was exploring other forms of thinking, living, and making work. I was tired of academia, perhaps precisely because I'd figured out how the game fundamentally worked. There was not enough pleasure in it. Something was missing.

Always obsessed by learning, by doing well, something didn't sit right. I had just spent several years writing a book about avant-garde communities and their promise of provisionality, heterogeneity, and collectivity as practised in their many underground and counter-cultural publications. Feminist, queer, and intersectional magazines, in particular, taught me about a type of learning and thinking that remains radically open to having one's mind, one's practice, and even one's life changed through dialogue with others. I couldn't come armed with my big theories, ready to impose them on these unruly forms. The magazines taught me how to read them. They humbled me. I repeatedly did not know them and let myself be guided by them. Towards the end of that book, I already knew that the formal experiments or emotional stakes so vividly present in any avant-garde project also needed to be part of criticism. To make it art.

Oscar Wilde hits the nail on the head in 'The Critic as Artist', when he asks us to regard criticism as creative:

> GILBERT: Why should it not be? It works with materials, and puts them into a form that is at once new and delightful. What more can one say of poetry? The critic will certainly be an interpreter, but he will not treat Art as a riddling Sphinx, whose shallow secret may be guessed and revealed by one whose feet are wounded and who knows not his name. Rather, he will look upon Art as a goddess whose mystery it is his

province to intensify, and whose majesty his privilege to make more marvellous in the eyes of men.

More than that: I wanted writing to be my beloved. For that, I needed to return to the drawing board. I needed to learn to write differently, again.

Writing, for me, gives form to reading. *Lessons of Decal*, therefore is, humbly and obsessively, a book that writes through its experience of reading and learning from that reading. Committed to the lessons that specific works teach me and to the many voices I conjure and bring into the room, I asked myself: how do I share that room with others, how do I make them feel the magic or resistance that I feel, which sometimes fashions fandom or recalcitrance or trance or stupor or delight or disgust? The book also traces my experiments with and attempts at understanding what it means to teach what I love.

Cusick, admirably, wants 'to increase the actual intimacy of my students' subsequent encounters with that music, or with any music, by increasing their knowledge of who it is, so to speak, who's been "on top," and by increasing their skill, through practice, in the art of being music's beloved.'[8] I fell in love with this promise for pedagogy. Like any lover, that means constantly negotiating desire, understanding, compassion, and change. As Cusick specifies, the type of work that allows this queer (listening) position is one in which 'I experience a continuous circulation of power': 'In all performances that give me joy, the answer is unclear—we are both on top, both on our backs, both wholly ourselves and wholly mingled with each other. Power circulates freely across porous boundaries; the categories player and played, lover and beloved, dissolve'.[9]

And that position requires a certain vulnerability, openness, and not-knowing-in-advance.

*

One Tuesday morning I talk to my students about 'not knowing', not knowing individually *and* in the classroom, as a social space we create together. We discuss what it might mean to practise a more experiential, non-extractive analysis (especially if we think of extraction as capitalist and colonial). Instead, as one of my students puts it, we can learn to describe when we are bored. When our thoughts wander.

That evening, a student emails me a playlist, describing how the music hooks a listener. And how we might translate this into other art practices.

I reply saying it would be productive to think about a phenomenology of hooks.

(Did I want them to think of fishhooks, the musical hook as some perverse pop abattoir, or of the more benign picture hooks, pitching art as attachment, a dangling suspension?)

I also ask: how do you marinate an essay?

(NB possible writing prompt—HOW TO MARINATE AN ESSAY, A LECTURE ON SOAKING TEXTS FOR TENDERNESS)

*

Thinking about the possibility of an intimate encounter with a work, for me, and for others, I return to these questions:

How do I render myself vulnerable in my work as a spur to new work? Can vulnerability be a route to a type of knowledge that I can't predict? How do I make myself open to uncertainty? Metaphorically, metaphysically, and practically. There is safety in the default. There is safety in distance. Being someone who doesn't accept straying from script, how do I square my obsessive perfectionism with a desire for a radical undoing, or the aspiration to remain open to the unexpected? How do I allow myself to 'not-know'? What would this vulnerable not-knowing mean in practice?

Of course, writing about vulnerability, as I'm doing here, doesn't make me vulnerable in the slightest. It's a performance. Not in the sense of 'pretentious' but as a medium, a genre. A choreographed doing that is staged and framed, by conventions, by discourse, by context, by repetition. It holds something up to view, for analysis. As my friend Seda wisely quipped on a train journey recently: 'Emotions are good because you can analyse them.'

This may be the right place to address the elephant in the room which is the credo that autobiographical work must somehow entail vulnerability. But what kind of vulnerability? I have very little patience for the soppy, the soapy. So-called autobiographical vulnerability is often very soapy. All soap, no bubbles.

Autobiographical or not, I want work to non-didactically teach me something about reading, writing, and making art. I care about work when it makes me want to write and make art too. Walter Benjamin argued in 'The Author as Producer' that a writer must have 'a teacher's attitude': 'A writer who does not teach other writers teaches nobody'. He continues: a writer's work or mode of working 'must have the character of a model'. The more readers a work turns into collaborators the better. One model that fulfilled this for Benjamin was Brecht's epic theatre. It makes people think and feel differently because it does something with and to Form.

Form is my side-kick.

'Form is the shape of my discontent' (Amy Sillman).[10]

I will make another concession. There's a specific type of autobiographical work I've always allowed myself—and permission is a key word in art and writing, because there's always an element of desire and approval, even if it means ignoring and shunting it—so what I will allow is fake autobiography. A fake autobiography maintains its truth claim, its foothold in reality, but throws in the lies of fiction. Granted, there can be a thrill of revelation, but I'm attracted to the thrill of abstraction. The thrill of revelation confirms and comforts me in showing me what I already knew or suspected. The thrill of abstraction is the intimation of something that I could not have known, the not-yet-there, not yours and not mine. Buzzing. It makes my nervous system fizz. It's as if something within me is tickled, in faint future understanding. As if my soft tissue or the cochlear or some other invisible part of my body understands, and my brain is playing constant catch-up.

Jenny Diski's deadpan unromantic approach to writing and memory resonates with me:

'Memory is continually created, a story told and retold, using jigsaw pieces of experience. It's utterly unreliable in some ways, because who can say whether the feeling or emotion that seems to belong to the recollection actually belongs to it rather than being available from the general store of likely emotions we have learned? Who can say that this image is correct, and not an image from a book or film or a picture, another part of one's life'.[11]

For me, this is a fascinating approach to reading. What does this say about my memory of reading? It becomes part of my life, so much so that it merges with my other memories and feelings. Reading is a feeling. I do probably give a specific book, artwork, or performance, some 'likely emotions [I] have learned'. Again, how do we give form to what moves and impresses us? Perhaps by building reading into the practice of writing.

As Brooke-Rose wrote so pugnaciously: 'An experience is not in itself of the slightest interest merely because it happened to oneself'. Interest, without getting too philosophical about it, is often attributed to the object—this work of art, this book, is *interesting*—when in reality interest is an activity that resides entirely within me. It requires my agency. I'm either taking an interest or I'm not. I can make anything interesting to myself if I want to! So interest is more wrapped up in desire than we perhaps would like to admit…

In Virginia Woolf's *The Waves*, Bernard (the writer) sighs: 'Life is not susceptible to the treatment we give it when we try to tell it.' Indeed: 'How tired I am of stories . . . I begin to long for some little language such as lovers use, broken words, inarticulate words, like the shuffling of feet upon the pavement.'

But actually: Life *is* susceptible. The act of telling, giving something over to speech does loop back. Because language opens up a space, pierces something and our lives are changed.

To be susceptible means to be
vulnerable
prone
liable
pre-disposed
inclined
open
receptive
impressionable

Oh you impressionable little thing. Did you really think
this was the real elephant at this eminent gathering?

I am prone to disagree.

For purely formal reasons. I enjoy a good argument
about form.

You are so hard to please.

I am otherwise inclined.

An incline is not yet steep. It's the first step to a hurdle. A
certain slant of light might do the trick. Rolls you down the
slope, like a tumbleweed. Or maybe you roll the big stone
up the hill, the hill that keeps on growing, the imagined
Sisyphean task.

Too much word play? Entertain me for a moment.
Synonyms are always near—that is, they're proximal, they're
approximations, projections. Like friends or lovers. And yet,
being next to something, there's always a degree of distance,
something that cannot be known.

What is this little language such as lovers use?

*

Why am I suddenly interested in vulnerability? Perhaps
because I want to surprise myself and I conjecture that a
certain type of vulnerability could get me there.

Etymologically, a now obsolete meaning of the word
'vulner-able' was: 'being able to wound'.

Eventually it changed from active to passive: being 'susceptible
to receiving wounds'.

For anything biographical you sometimes hedge your
words. Shakespeare's sonnet 94 is famously ambiguous in
its treatment of vulnerability:

'They that have pow'r to hurt and will do none,
That do not do the thing they most do show,
Who, moving others, are themselves as stone,
Unmovèd, cold, and to temptation slow' (94.1-4)

There's such theatrical distance built into this poem and yet
I am shocked that 'they' can move others but are themselves
'as stone'? To move others do I have to be immune to being
moved? Do we praise or deride that? Giddying between self-
containment and looseness, knowledge and uncertainty.

How do we 'not do the thing [we] must do show'? The thing
'they' most show is their power to hurt which they never
exercise. Is this line also related to desire? Why is it admirable
to *not* be easily tempted ('to temptation slow')? For a long time,
as a lover of Difficulty, I would have agreed. But now I *do* want

to be tempted, want to be everything *but* 'unmovèd, cold'.

*

I had a realisation recently in a singing lesson—I am not
drawn to difficult words purely for their difficulty. I am
drawn to difficult words because my feelings towards
them and my knowledge of them are often not previously
determined. I can suck on them for hours, making the
lozenges smaller and smaller until their core has left an
imprint on my tongue. I don't feel bound by their prior
meaning, they're not loaded with cliché. A difficult word,
with its imprint on my tongue, its decal on my palate, can
express feeling without me putting it there. I think that's
a form of aesthetics—it has nothing to do with pretence
and everything to do with touch and curiosity. Maybe this
is how vulnerability and difficulty and autobiography find
their common ground, their resolution: maybe the way to
overcome my suspicion of autobiography is to look for it
elsewhere. Maybe it lies in an embodied response or in a
formal experiment. In abstraction I can be myself. I learn
something about myself, without having to say what it is. I
can remain unknown to myself. And yet in that unknowing, I
begin to cotton onto myself.

*

Plangent is a difficult word I once looked up and then forgot
the meaning of. I thought it meant pleasing. Maybe because
it's often used to describe music. The plangent oboe. But
plangent is the reverberating beat of lament, the loud
formula of melancholy. Like the breaking waves pulling you
under. Like a plunge into the unknown.

[1] The decal can also be found etymologically in papier calque, which is 'tracing paper', where the original shimmers through.

[2] Kathy Acker, 'Devoured by Myths: An Interview with Sylvère Lotringer', in *Hannibal Lecter, My Father* (New York: Semiotext(e), 2001), pp. 7, 11.

[3] I first used this line in a video piece with Kate Clayton, *Pearl & Theory Make Compost* (2020).

[4] Brooke-Rose, *Invisible Author: Last Essays* (Columbus: Ohio State University Press, 2002), p. 178.

[5] Brooke-Rose, *Invisible Author*, p. 1.

[6] William Empson, *Some Versions of Pastoral* (New Directions, 1935), p. 77.

[7] Suzanne Cusick, 'On A Lesbian Relationship with Music: A Serious Effort Not to Think Straight', in *Queering the Pitch: The New Lesbian and Gay Musicology*, ed. by Elizabeth Wood and Philip Brett (New York: Routledge, 2006), 67–83.

[8] Cusick, 'On a Lesbian Relationship with Music', p. 74.

[9] Cusick, 'On a Lesbian Relationship with Music', p. 78.

[10] Amy Sillman, *Faux Pas: Selected Writings & Drawings* (expanded edition) (After 8 Books, 2022), p. 164.

[11] Jenny Diski, *Skating to Antarctica* (Virago), p. 147.

Acknowledgements

A textile swatch is a small piece of fabric that stands in for a larger whole. Swatches allow an artist to see how different materials look and feel before making a decision to use them in a final piece. Language is a kind of swatch.

My friends—thank you for holding up the language swatch for me. Without dialogue—this book wouldn't have been possible. Specifically, Kat Addis, for introducing me to the pentimento, for deep chats about haberdashery, hems, and poetic indulgence, and Yates Norton—for making me take out all the unnecessary frills in some places and revel in baroque ornamentation in others. You both put the 'close' back into close reading. Wendy, for allowing me to 'use' her words both tenderly and pruriently, knowing that this form of *too-close* reading is an act of admiration and friendship. Also, over the years: Adam Moore, Alice Butler, Anna Moschovakis, Carol Szymanski, Chana Morgenstern, Claudia Tobin, Dorothy Wang, Ella Finer, Emma Attwood, Emma Gomis, Erin Robinsong, lee rae walsh, Kate Clayton, Lucy van de Wiel, Naomi Woo, Sarah Hayden, Sawako Nakayasu, Seda Ergul, Simone Kearney, Uljana Wolf, Yael Ort-Dinoor, Youngsook Choi—for conversation, for listening, for inspiration, for push-back, for encouragement.

Thank you to all the editors, curators, and institutions that invited me to write or present the pieces that appear here. These occasions and invitations were invaluable in teasing out ideas, letting me 'think into a room', and wait for an echo. Azad and Kashif, and everyone at the 87 Press, have thoughtfully shepherded this book into production, and I want to honour their commitment to experimental publishing.

Many of the ideas presented here have percolated since I first trialled them by pouring them out tentatively, or performatively, or profusely, into the space that is the classroom. I therefore want to thank my students, both past and present, who taught me that teaching is also a creative practice.

Laura, the ultimate reader, to whom everything is addressed, whose voice shimmers through all these words. Cosmo, canine teacher par excellence, has shown me how to know simple joy.

You all remind me that friendship and love are forms of reading one another, tirelessly, endlessly, pointing out when the traces and layers show too much or too little or in just the right way.

Lastly, to those who taught me, perhaps without knowing, and who exceed the perimeters of what this book might touch—I still feel your imprint.